HOLIDAYS AND FESTIVALS

Memorial Day

Rebecca Rissman

Heinemann Library
Chicago, Illinois

www.heinemannraintree.com
Visit our website to find out more information about Heinemann-Raintree books.

To order:

☎ Phone 888-454-2279

💻 Visit www.heinemannraintree.com to browse our catalog and order online.

Edited by Adrian Vigliano and Rebecca Rissman
Designed by Ryan Frieson
Picture research by Tracy Cummins
Leveling by Nancy E. Harris
Originated by Capstone Global Library Ltd.
Printed in China by South China Printing Company Ltd.

15 14 13 12 11 10
10 9 8 7 6 5 4 3 2 1

Library of Congress Cataloging-in-Publication Data
Rissman, Rebecca.
 Memorial Day / Rebecca Rissman.
  p. cm.—(Holidays and festivals)
 Includes bibliographical references and index.
 ISBN 978-1-4329-4054-6 (hc)—ISBN 978-1-4329-4073-7 (pb) 1.
Memorial Day—Juvenile literature. I. Title.
 E642.R57 2011
 394.262—dc22
                                    2009052854

Acknowledgments

The author and publishers are grateful to the following for permission to reproduce copyright material: AP Photo/Lisa Poole **p.4**; AP Photo/Chris Gardner **p.19**; Corbis ©Michael Reynolds/EPA **p.5**; Corbis ©Jim Young/Reuters **p.15**; Corbis ©Ariel Skelley **p.18**; Corbis ©Jay Syverson **p.21**; Corbis ©Jim Young/Reuters **p.23c**; Getty Images **p.8**; Getty Images/MPI **p.10**; Getty Images/Brendan Smialowski **p.16**; Getty Images/KAREN BLEIER/AFP **p.17**; Getty Images/KAREN BLEIER/AFP **p.23a**; Getty Images **p.23b**; istockphoto ©John Clines **p.22**; Library of Congress Prints and Photographs Division **pp.7**, **11**, **23d**; National Archive **p.9**; Shutterstock ©Jeremy R. Smith Sr. **p.14**; Shutterstock ©Lee Prince **p.20**; The Granger Collection, New York **pp.6**, **12**, **13**.

Cover photograph of American flags placed on gravestones in Arlington, VA reproduced with permission of Getty Images/Mark Wilson. Back cover photograph reproduced with permission of Shutterstock ©Jeremy R. Smith Sr.

Every effort has been made to contact copyright holders of any material reproduced in this book. Any omissions will be rectified in subsequent printings if notice is given to the publisher.

Contents

What Is a Holiday?

People celebrate holidays.
A holiday is a special day.

Memorial Day is a holiday.
Memorial Day is in May.

The Story of Memorial Day

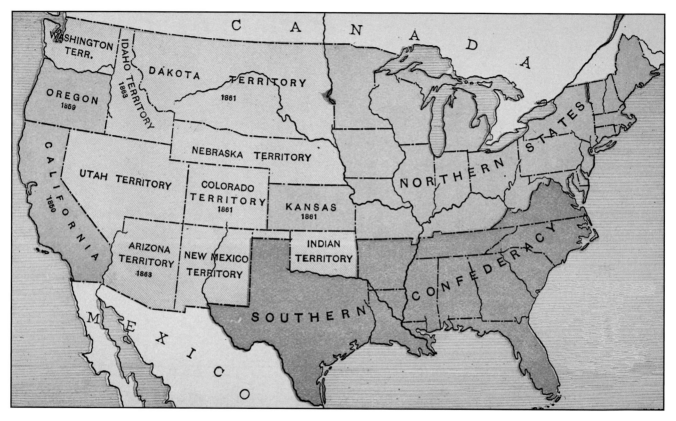

 In 1860 two parts of America fought each other. The two parts were the North and the South.

This fight was called the Civil War.

The South wanted to become a new country. The South wanted to have slaves.

The North did not want the South to become a new country. The North wanted to free the slaves.

In 1865 the North won the war. The slaves were free.

Many Americans died in the war. People in the North and the South were very sad.

People put flowers on the graves of soldiers from the North and the South.

The people showed that they
were thankful for what the soldiers
had done.

Celebrating Memorial Day

On Memorial Day people remember soldiers who died fighting for the United States.

14

People give thanks for soldiers.

People leave flags and flowers
on graves.

People fly the American flag at half-mast to honor soldiers.

People come together to listen to music and eat food.

People think and talk about the
United States.

Memorial Day Symbols

The American flag is a symbol of Memorial Day.

Graves decorated with flowers and flags are symbols of Memorial Day.

Calendar

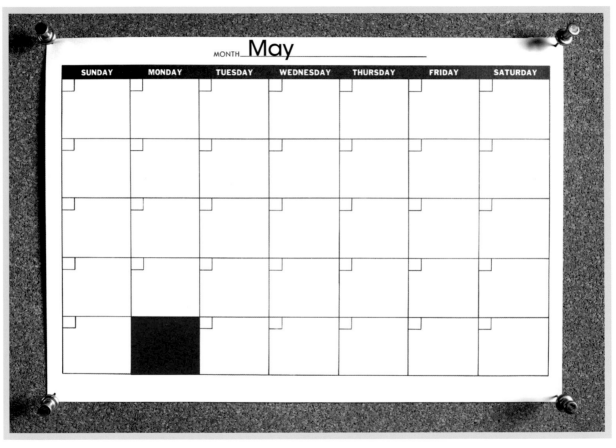

Memorial Day is the last Monday in May.

Picture Glossary

 **half-mast** when flags are flown in the middle of a flagpole

 **slaves** people who are forced to work for no pay

 **soldiers** people who serve in the military

 **war** a fight between two or more countries or groups

Index

Note to Parents and Teachers

Before reading

Briefly explain the armed forces including the five branches. Explain that every May Americans recognize Memorial Day, a special day when we remember those who have lost their lives in war. Some children will have personal experience with family or friends who currently serve in the military or have been killed in battle. For others, death will still be a more abstract concept. Allow the children to talk about these experiences.

After reading

Using art supplies and butcher paper, create a wall of remembrance. Have the children draw pictures and write words of people, pets, or events that have passed that they want to remember. Explain that remembering is another way we "memorialize" something or someone.

The Lifelong Gardener

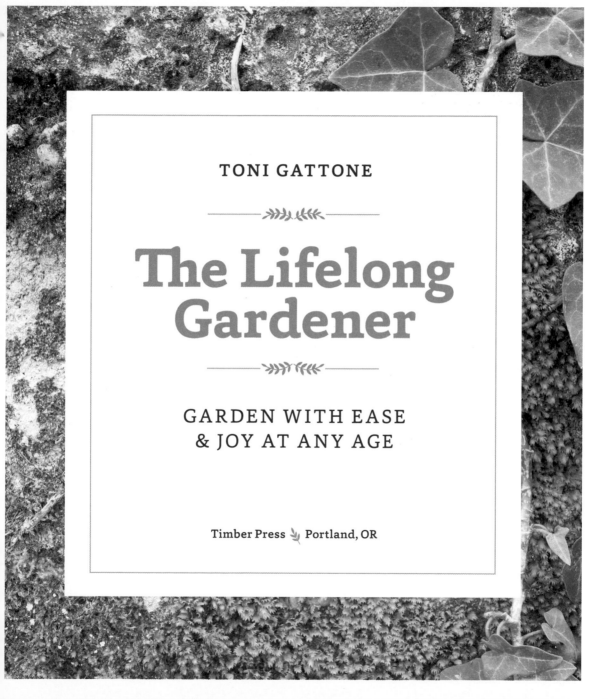

TONI GATTONE

The Lifelong Gardener

GARDEN WITH EASE & JOY AT ANY AGE

Timber Press · Portland, OR

Published in 2019 by Timber Press, Inc.
The Haseltine Building
133 S.W. Second Avenue, Suite 450
Portland, Oregon 97204-3527
timberpress.com

Printed in China

Text design by Kelley Galbreath
Cover design by Kim Thwaits

ISBN: 978-1-60469-853-4

Catalog records for this book are available from the
Library of Congress and the British Library.

I AM BLESSED WITH A LARGE LOVING ITALIAN FAMILY and many friends who gave me the confidence to follow my dreams and to complete this book.

My Mom, Giovanna Jiampa Gattone, (also known as Jaye), was the first to see me and love me unconditionally. She always told me I could do whatever I set my mind to do. Mom was graced with an extraordinarily kind, caring, and generous heart. She was a great cook, and everyone who knew her, loved her. Thanks, Mom. In retrospect, the bad back I inherited from you led me to this adaptive gardening path.

I would not be who I am, or where I am today, if it weren't for the love and support my husband, Tim King, has given me over three decades of joyful married life. Tim saw the potential in me before I did, and with his wicked sense of humor, he reminded me not to take myself too seriously. He is the "King of Being," and I am the "Queen of Doing." While writing this book, I might have starved if it weren't for him bringing me lunch and making sure I had a cocktail or glass of wine at five o'clock. Thank you, Tim. You are the true joy of my life. I could not have done this without you. 143.

My sisters, Carole Gattone Arliskas and Dianne Gattone, have been cheering me on throughout the years, even as I continued to be a seeker—something they didn't always understand, but respected. Once I removed the nail from my foot that kept me going around in circles, I found my path, and they were there beside me, celebrating each milestone with love and joy.

Close and long-term friends, Nancy Harvey, Ellie Mitchell, Judith Henderson, Bren Taylor, Barbara Luttig-Haber, Carla Daro, Karen Turcotte, Bob Lasser, John Williams, and Lindsay Laven, thank you for your support, love, and friendship over so many years. You listened when I needed you and cheered me on.

Friends in my local Marin Master Gardener chapter, thank you for all the stories you shared with me when you discovered your own "new normal" in your garden and for all your suggestions on tools and techniques that worked for you. To Pat Randolph and Alanna Brady, thank you for believing in me and giving me the opportunity to present my adaptive gardening talk to our community at public seminars. That reinvigorated my speaking career.

Last but certainly not least, to my dear friend, Heidi Hornberger, who jumped in with two feet to be, first, my photographer, then my collaborator for this book. Thank you, Heidi, for your keen eye, your renewed love of gardening, and your joyful approach to life. You made this project one of laughter, ease, and gratitude.

Mille Grazie!

Contents

Preface

THE YEAR I BECAME A MASTER GARDENER, I couldn't wait to apply the information I'd learned so I could transform my garden. With my bad back, I knew the last thing I should be doing was wrestling with heavy things—like this *one* concrete pot I wanted to move—but I did it anyway.

For more than a week after, I was flat on my back and could barely walk. Getting out to my garden was impossible.

Laid out on my sofa, I could see my roses needed deadheading, but the pain was so bad, all I could do was take another pill.

Two weeks later, I was still on my back. I felt useless and was beginning to feel sorry for myself. I decided I had to find some way to adapt so I could garden again.

As soon as I thought the word "adapt," a light bulb went off in my head! On a recent trip to Oregon, I'd read an article on adaptive gardening in a newspaper called *Boomer and Senior News*. I remembered commenting to my husband, Tim, "Isn't that redundant? I mean: Boomers *and* seniors?"

I took another pain pill so I could get off the darned sofa. Bracing myself on furniture and door frames, I set off on a mission to find that article in my office at the other end of the house. I looked everywhere, through every file and drawer, until by some miracle, I found it.

It told the story of two women in Oregon who were helping seniors adapt their gardens to accommodate their changing ability levels. The women's clients wanted to ensure they could continue with their passion despite their aches and pains. I could relate to that. My own physical limitations seemed to be growing—I knew my back problem was chronic, and I didn't want to stop gardening. One particular line in the article stuck with me: "Garden smarter, not harder, so you can garden for life." Bingo!

I spent the rest of my sofa time with my laptop on my stomach, researching adaptive gardening. I found out there are 78 million boomers on their way to becoming seniors and felt like screaming from the rooftop when I realized: "I'm not alone!"

Eventually my back healed and I went back to work. After a few months of working with Master Gardeners, I wanted to find a way to share my love of gardening with my community, so I started presenting public seminars like *Edible Landscaping* and *Growing Edibles in Containers*. I noticed right away that the majority of our audiences were seniors. It turns out, Marin County is one of the oldest populations in California—one in four residents is over sixty years old. I envisioned being of service to those seniors and gardeners with limited mobility issues, by helping them understand how they could adapt their gardens now so they wouldn't have to re-do them or (worse) abandon them later.

I feel grateful to have the opportunity to share this important message with you. Thank you, Stacee Gravelle Lawrence, acquisitions editor at Timber Press, for calling me after hearing my presentation at the Northwest Flower & Garden Show in Seattle and asking if I'd be interested in writing this book. What a life-changing journey this has been.

My generation, the Boomers, doesn't want to give up the things we love just because we're getting older. NEVER GIVE UP is our motto. My purpose for writing this book is to share what I have learned about how to keep gardening, even when your back or knees are screaming at you.

Come with me, as we walk the path of adaptive gardening together. No matter what happens, we will never give up what feeds our soul.

Introduction

Salute! Here's to Your Health

Gardening is one of the healthiest activities for anyone, but especially for seniors. It gets you out of the house, into nature and fresh air. It also involves bending and stretching, which can help with flexibility and balance, increasing your strength and ultimately, your range of motion.

For those of us who have received our AARP card, a routine activity, such as a bit of gardening every day, can reduce the risk of stroke and promote a longer, healthier life. Researchers for *British Journal of Sports Medicine* followed a group of 4,000 sixty year olds in Stockholm, Sweden, for twelve years. Those with the highest level of daily physical activity had 27 percent lower risk of heart attack or stroke, and 30 percent reduced risk of death from all causes.

The bottom line is that we all love to garden—yet many of the chores, like raking, weeding, pruning, digging, and even harvesting, can play havoc with our bodies.

Drum roll, please . . . adaptive gardening, to the rescue!

I find the love of gardening grows upon me more and more as I grow older.

MARIA EDGEWORTH

What Is Adaptive Gardening?

Adaptive gardening offers dozens of ways for gardeners of all ages with a limited range of motion, the wheelchair bound, or anyone wanting to reduce stress on their joints, to identify what works for them in their garden according to their personal physical realities.

I bring nearly thirty years of experience to this kind of problem solving. The business I started in 1990, Toni Gattone & Associates, has given me great opportunity to find the best ergonomic tools in an ever-changing garden market. My approach will help you think through what you may need in the future, so you can make changes now and not have to undo your hard work later.

The objectives of adaptive gardening are threefold:

1 To raise awareness of adaptive techniques that enable garden-ers to re-think how and when they garden for greater ease.

2 To describe ways gardens can be changed or modified to ensure the safety and comfort of the gardener.

3 To modify favorite tools to increase their usability or to replace them with more ergonomic options.

WHY DO YOU NEED IT?

We have all been given a gift. Did you know the average life expectancy in the United States has grown by thirty-years during the past century alone? That's good to know because we all want to thrive in our lives, and living longer means we have more time to do the things we love. We are all pioneers finding new ways to live vital, meaningful, and happy lives into our seventies, eighties, nineties, and beyond.

Research shows that happy adults usually have a support group of like-minded individuals. Luckily, garden clubs abound. Happy adults

10 ADAPTIVE GARDENING RULES TO LIVE BY

1 Our bodies change. That's life. When we realize we have limitations that stop us from doing what we want to do, we have to learn to "accept what is" first. Then, and only then, can we develop resiliency by looking for other ways to get it done.

2 You deserve a safe and comfortable garden to work in.

3 One of the best things you can do for your body is to stretch, stretch, stretch before you start gardening. Do yoga, tai chi, or dance to some upbeat music that gets you moving and warmed up.

4 Switch it up! This keeps things interesting and saves you energy. Every thirty minutes, start a different chore using a different part of the body. It's repetitive movement that causes pain, so switching it up will keep you from feeling sore the next day.

5 When you garden smarter, it takes less time to do more. Anticipate the chores you plan on doing and decide what tools and gloves you will need. Then grab a tote and bring your tools to the job, so you won't have to double back for "one more thing."

6 Save time and money by planting perennials or shrubs rather than annuals. By using the concept of "right plant, right place," you won't be making costly mistakes buying a fig tree that wants to be thirty feet tall when you only have room for a dwarf.

7 Don't be afraid to ask for help. Make sure your requests are specific and you include a deadline for any help you hire. Have more fun by inviting friends over to help. If you grow succulents, let them take home pups you have propagated. From your garden to theirs—everybody wins!

8 Look for ways to make your gardening life easy. When you buy new containers, make them self-watering. Buy a tool sharpener so every cut you make is with a sharp pruner.

9 Only use ergonomic tools that are comfortable to use. Adapted tools are easy to create and cost pennies on the dollar compared to new tools.

10 If you have a bad back, it is pure joy to stand up and garden. Find eye-level vertical gardening opportunities. Then stand back to admire your work.

are also passionate about something they enjoy doing. Well, gardening is one hobby millions of people are passionate about. Gardeners love nothing more than to spend time in our gardens—actually, being in any garden, anywhere, makes us happy.

But however much we love to garden, back, knee, shoulder, or hip pain doesn't make it easy. You may have thought you might have to give it up, or at a minimum, find new ways to approach it. If you learn to adapt, gardening can bring you joy for the rest of your life.

WHO NEEDS IT?

Seniors and gardeners of any age who have limited mobility or physical issues, as well as children and caretakers of senior gardeners, can benefit from adaptive gardening.

I remember reading a story about a woman who thought she would have to give up gardening altogether due to her limited mobility issues, but she now has her caregiver helping her maintain her herb garden and the food growing in her raised beds. With her caregiver's help, she's still able to feel the joy that comes from doing what she loves, which is being in her garden. She's not doing all of the work herself, but she is enjoying teaching someone else. She could have thrown in the towel and said, "I can't garden anymore because it has become too hard for me to do it alone." Instead, she found a way to get it done.

I believe there's always another way to get it done. We must be resilient and resourceful. Believe in yourself and do what makes you happy.

WHEN SHOULD YOU START?

Now! Start where you are. Think about what hurts you when you garden. Decide what chores have become increasingly difficult to do. Then take a hard look at your garden and plan for whatever the future may hold.

Let's face it, we are living in a stressful and complicated world. All the more reason to take time to get down to earth. As I write this in the fall of 2018, I'm struck by how different our world is from just a few years ago. If watching the news makes you crazy, why not spend more time in your garden to shift your gears?

Years ago, I had a high energy sales job and worked for an insecure sales manager who enjoyed pulling the rug out from under me as a way of testing me. I was super stressed, and when I got home from work, I would pour myself a glass of wine, grab my pruners, and go out into my garden.

What began as a little dead-heading often resulted in creating a beautiful bouquet of roses and cut flowers to bring indoors. Still in my business suit, my stress melted away, and it was replaced with a feeling of joy. Gardening has always been an attitude adjustment for me and if you are reading this book, I'm betting you feel the same.

Seasons change. Storms come and go. Changes will occur. This is a certainty. No matter your age or your abilities, we have to roll with the punches as life runs its course and find solutions to whatever we think is holding us back.

How To Use This Book

I prefer not to dwell on physical challenges but instead to focus on proactive solutions to those challenges. Many of the tips, tools, and techniques I've outlined in this book have check boxes beside them, so you can mark and then later easily find the information that resonates with you whenever you need it.

Some of the tips may not resonate with every gardener. We are all so different, and we all approach gardening from a different mindset, not to mention numerous growing zones and microclimates. Just as there are no two gardens alike anywhere in the world, there are no two gardeners alike. Each of us chooses what will work for us in our gardens. Take what works for you and pass on tips to friends who may need them. Sharing knowledge makes a better world for us all.

YOU & YOUR BODY

Old age is always fifteen years older than I am.

OLIVER WENDELL HOLMES

Daily "Be" Attitudes

You love to garden, and always have. Don't stop now. The single most important thing you can do is to adjust your attitude. The older I get, the more I find simply *being* serves me better than obsessing about doing.

Be in a "glass half full" state of mind

Be active and keep moving

Be willing to let go

Be resilient

Be sustainable; grow your own food

Be humble enough to ask for help

Be good to your body

Be generous with your community

Be open to gardening together with friends

Be proactive about creating opportunities for ease

Believe you can, and you can

Be joyful

TONI'S TIP

Identify what you can control versus what is outside of your control. Remember that sometimes the only thing you have control over is your attitude!

Change your attitude by coming to grips with the reality of whatever limited mobility issues and/or physical challenges you may be experiencing. Find ways to transform your pain into joy. I believe in adapting to our lives as we age. After all, it's not how long we'll live, but how well.

Accept What Is

You are reading this book because you have a love for gardening and you don't intend to stop—even though you've noticed changes in your body are affecting your ability to keep up with your garden. Before you read another word, know that my intent here is to help you get to a place of accepting these changes for what they are. Especially in the case of getting older, it's not about your years, it's about how you feel.

Many equate aging with powerlessness, but the truth is we can be role models for one another and for those who come after us. For gardeners, passing on our knowledge and our passion for gardening feeds our souls as much as tending our own yards.

What happens when mobility issues become apparent, or you start to experience physical concerns that keep you from comfortably working in your garden? What happens when gardening becomes more painful than joyful?

Be honest as you ask yourself some questions:

1 What body movements cause you pain?

2 What garden chores have become too difficult to do anymore?

3 What garden jobs can you continue to do on your own?

4 What chores can you delegate to someone in your household or someone you hire?

5 How can you modify the everyday and seasonal garden chores that still need to be done?

Your New Normal

If you're like me, gone are those long weekends when you could be out gardening all day and nothing bothered you. Now there are days when you cannot garden for more than an hour or two at a time. We have all dealt with these moments of reckoning. Perhaps it was the first time you said to yourself, "Oops! What just happened? Did I trip on something, or was my balance off?" Whatever the red flag, you realize you're dealing with a "new normal" when it comes to tasks you can complete in comfort, without pain or hazard.

Take responsibility for accepting this reality. You cannot change your situation or undo your mobility issues, but you can change your view. As my mom used to say: "It is what it is. You might as well accept it." Aging is a natural process we all go through. Train your thoughts on the positives in your life and the things you can do that bring you joy. Be creative.

Ask yourself: How can I cultivate a new way of looking at growing older? How can I make friends with my body the way it is now? How can I modify my approach to gardening so I can give up what no longer works, in order to focus on what is important? Giving up a chore like climbing a ladder to trim hedges can be redeeming if you devote your energy instead to something you find rewarding, like planting containers filled with veggies and herbs for your family to enjoy.

We change our relationship with change by changing our attitude toward it. We change our attitude by changing our perspective and how we view it, how we speak about it, and ultimately, how we live through it.

Here are several lifestyle modifications that can change your attitude toward your new normal:

☐ *Keep moving. Strive for thirty minutes a day do some kind of cardiovascular exercise. Get off the sofa and into the garden. Be in nature. Find activities you love and do them several times a week. Just keep moving!*

☐ *Change your attitude by changing your environment. Get out of town! Going to new places can give you what you're looking for, even if just for a weekend. My advice is to include a visit to a beautiful garden where you can recharge, relax, and get inspired.*

☐ *Get a good sleep each night.*

☐ *Create time to be—meditate or seek other stress-relieving activities. We live in a complicated world, take time to be still. Everyone should have a place in their garden dedicated to simply sitting still and listening to nature.*

☐ *Grow your community. Keep socially active to remind yourself you're not alone. Take your love of growing roses, irises, or begonias and join a garden club to fuel your passion for gardening.*

- [ ] *Take a class. Join a book club. Become a Master Gardener. If you think you don't know enough, or if the idea of learning something new is daunting, get a friend to go with you.*

- [ ] *Take cues from someone who is already resilient and start a conversation with them. Ask them how they got past their health issues. Let go of negative people, and make room for positive ones to come into your life.*

- [ ] *Recognize what makes you unique and think about areas where you are confident and strong. Own it.*

- [ ] *Be willing to change, even if you're not sure how.*

- [ ] *Don't focus on your age. The actual number of years you have been walking on earth doesn't mean anything, except in your head. You can look around and find gardeners much older than you working in their yards day after day.*

Expect Ease

How can you get to a place of looking for peace or ease, at every intersection? How do we get to "ease" when our back, hips, or wrists are bellowing?

I'm convinced if you focus your attention on things being easy, rather than getting caught up in ways a chore or an event is going to be hard, be easy they will. Think about and expect ease at every turn. Ask yourself: "How can I make this easier?"

Here are a few other easy ideas:

☐ *Expect ease. Before every chore, every phone call, every event, expect it will happen with harmony and have the "most benevolent outcome" (MBO).*

☐ *Done is better than perfect. Some of us tend to make things harder than they need to be, and we struggle by tweaking and re-tweaking, working and reworking our gardens. Develop the philosophy: done is better than perfect. It's hard, but then you can sit in your garden and enjoy it.*

After a hard day's work, take it easy.

GARDENER PROFILE

NO TWO ALIKE

I **'VE HEARD GARDENERS SAY** they would rather die than not be able to continue gardening. One friend told me she would be at a complete loss if she couldn't garden.

As there are no two gardens alike, there are no two gardeners who have the same abilities or disabilities. Each gardener must assess their gardens and their abilities as they are today and as they may become in the foreseeable future. Even a small change can throw us off balance. We must be resilient and accept our "new normal" by figuring out new ways to get things done.

My friend used to enjoy spreading a thick layer of mulch around her garden every spring. She knew it would help conserve water and keep out weeds, and she loved it as the finishing touch to her garden. She described it as "putting the frame around the picture."

Now, because of limited mobility in her shoulder, hauling heavy bags of mulch has become too much of an undertaking. Fortunately, my friend didn't deny or resist, and while it took her a while to get there, she learned to accept her new norm, which involved hiring a helper to distribute the mulch, leaving plenty of other fun tasks for her to do on her own.

Know Your Limits

Know your limits, what you can and cannot do, and know when to say:

BASTA!

Basta means "Enough!" in Italian. My mom used to say that to us when we were making too much noise or wanted a second bottle of Coke. And when she was done planting her tomatoes, she'd finish by declaring, "Basta!"

If *Basta* doesn't resonate with you, you can cry "Uncle!" or find some ritual associated with moving on. There's always something to do in the garden, so attack the elephant one toenail at a time. Accept you may not get the entire project completed in one day but you can devote time each day, until it is done.

Resilience Is Everything

Resilience is your ability to adapt well and recover quickly after setbacks, loss, trauma, or tragedy. If you have a resilient disposition, you're better able to maintain poise and a healthy level of physical and psychological wellness in the face of life's challenges. According to the Mayo Clinic, those who are less resilient are more likely to dwell on problems, feel victimized, become overwhelmed, use unhealthy coping tactics to handle stress, and develop anxiety and depression.

Resilience won't make your problems go away—but it can help you to see past them, find joy in life, and handle setbacks when they strike. You may still feel anger, grief, disappointment, and pain, but you can keep functioning, which is the most important thing.

OPPOSITE: *"I know I shouldn't be getting on that ladder. . ."*

Aging is an issue of mind over matter.
If you don't mind, it doesn't matter.

MARK TWAIN

Physical changes in our bodies, a financial crisis, the loss of a special person in our lives—these are all stressful experiences that

can leave you feeling exhausted and questioning your ability to keep going. Gardening can be a powerful healing tool at these times. When fellow Master Gardener and landscaper Tony Mekisich experienced a huge personal loss, he found planning a new garden, working with his hands, and creating something beautiful filled his heart and gave him something to look forward to each day.

It is important to strengthen our resilience to discomfort, as a path to inner peace. We cannot stop the external course of things and how they show up in our lives, because we have no control of what happens in our lives, but we do have control of how we respond. Instead of letting our discomfort derail us, we can train ourselves so we are more resistant to it.

You must trust this truth—no matter how you feel right now, in time, you will find your way back to center. Until then, be patient and gentle with yourself, practice self-compassion and self-care. If there is one thing I know for sure, resilience is a skill that can be learned, and it will help you pick yourself up, dust yourself off, and start all over again.

Keep in Mind

Many of us will keep our problems to ourselves, or try to figure it out on our own, but actually, reaching out to others for support is a huge part of becoming resilient.

IN OCTOBER 2017, MASSIVE WILDFIRES ripped across Northern California, burning parts of Napa, Sonoma, and Lake counties. By the time it was finally extinguished, the fire had killed forty-three people and burned over 36,000 acres. At the time, it was considered to be the most destructive fire in our state's history.

And yet, after the fire, sights like in the image above were common. These hazelnut trees in the Glen Ellen area of Sonoma County are resprouting after nearly burning away in the fire. Nature is ever-resilient and so are we.

In order to pull through to a happy life filled with ease and joy, we must learn to recover and bounce back after illness, tragedy, and loss. We must find resiliency in our day to day lives.

Remember, You're Not Alone

If you are a Baby Boomer, you were born any year from 1946 to 1964, and I'm here to tell you, you are certainly not alone. Since January, 2011, 78 million Baby Boomers, the largest, most active generation ever born, have turned sixty-five. That is 10,000 per day, 4 million per year.

The number of Americans over sixty-five will nearly triple by 2030. There will also be nine million people over eighty-five. Worldwide, the number of those age sixty and over is expected to double by 2050, and triple by 2100—the older population will be increasing by 800,000 every thirty days.

Public health officials and economists have been warning of the imminent arrival of the "Silver Tsunami." By 2050, all surviving Baby Boomers will be over the age of eighty-five. When I went through the Master Gardener program, I was blown away when I discovered our chapter had more than 350 active members, and a large percentage were retired or near retirement. It brought me comfort to know I wasn't alone in many of my struggles.

As more and more Boomers are newly retired, they must rethink and alter how ordinary tasks are done. Arthritis and deteriorating joints from a lifetime of sports and exercise is forcing Boomers to face their growing limitations. For avid gardeners, surrendering our passion isn't an option. Instead, we are looking for ways to make our gardens more comfortable, safe, and accessible during our golden years, allowing us to continue gardening for years to come.

Keep in Mind

Most of what people think of as aging can be slowed with exercise, having an active social life, and gardening. And guess what? Combining all three is the perfect way to offset aging issues!

Pain can change you, but that doesn't mean it has to be a bad change. Take that pain and turn it into wisdom.

DALAI LAMA

Our Changing Bodies

Seniors report all kinds of changes in their bodies as they age. How you react to those changes can make all the difference in how you live your life. Many people in their nineties still work in their gardens, as do those with physical handicaps or disabilities. Know your options and garden smart. Gardening with physical limitations is not only possible, it is a great way to maintain your lifestyle during a time of physical adjustment. Creating a garden that is suited to your specific needs is an important part of your journey.

Below are some general tips for success in the garden despite physical challenges you may be experiencing. Following this, you'll find a list of common ways our bodies change and a few ideas for adapting in the garden.

☐ *No matter your physical constraints, warm up your muscles and joints before gardening and do light stretching to reduce soreness afterwards.*

☐ *Besides eating well, walking is the single most important thing we can do for ourselves. It gets blood flowing and helps with our balance.*

☐ *No one over sixty should be using a ladder. Replace ladders with sturdy stepstools that have a grab bar at the top. Never stand on the highest step.*

☐ *Carry your cell phone with you when you're in the garden, just in case.*

BALANCE

Balance can be an issue as we age. Here are some modifications you can make in the garden if balance is your concern:

☐ *All walking surfaces should be solid, smooth, and level to eliminate tripping hazards.*

☐ *Sit down to work in the garden.*

☐ *Give up getting on a ladder to trim trees and hedges.*

☐ *Clear clutter from all areas of your garden.*

☐ *Put away hoses after you use them.*

☐ *If you use a walker, add a pouch for carrying tools.*

☐ *Have handrails professionally installed.*

LEFT: *Your days carrying heavy bags of mulch or compost may be over, but there are ways to work around tasks like this.*

RIGHT: *A sturdy stepstool is much more suited to adaptive gardening than a ladder.*

STAMINA

There was a saying in our family we'd hear when someone was low energy: *E' come il pane sensa sole*. It's like bread without salt.

Low stamina can have a big impact on your motivation. You might not want to continue gardening if you don't have the energy to finish the job or if the work seems too vast. To keep yourself going, try these methods:

☐ *Break down big projects into smaller parts and work a little bit every day to get them done.*

☐ *Ask a friend to help.*

☐ *Provide yourself a seat to reduce distances and grades. Place seating in the shade.*

☐ *Keep tools and a water bottle nearby to cut down on extra movement and conserve energy.*

EXERCISES TO IMPROVE YOUR BALANCE:

☐ Practice standing on one foot when you are in line at the grocery store or while you wash dishes or brush your teeth.

☐ Incorporate a focused heel-to-toe walking, what some people call the sobriety walk, with one foot in front of the other and if you dare, with your eyes closed.

MOBILITY

Limited mobility (of any kind) makes it difficult to get around your garden to work. If you can no longer reach across your garden beds or carry heavy bags of compost or mulch, you may get discouraged. Don't quit. Learn your limits and find solutions to help. Long-reach and ease-of-use tools are particularly helpful for gardeners who can't bend, reach, and lift like they used to.

REACTION TIME

If your reflexes are slower than they once were, delegate the use of all power tools, like hedge trimmers, tillers, and chain saws to someone else and avoid preventable mishaps.

BACK PAIN

The numbers differ widely but it has been said as many as 75 percent of all gardeners have chronic back pain. It's comforting to know we're not alone.

☐ *Keep your back straight when you dig. Stay close to the blade when pushing the shovel into the soil and don't overload it.*

☐ *Find no-bend methods and tools for planting seeds and bulbs.*

☐ *Sit while you work. Keep a lightweight chair that's easy to move next to your containers and raised beds. Try a reversible kneeler seat or a rolling garden seat.*

☐ *Speak with your doctor about starting a back-strengthening program. Focus on core muscles.*

☐ *Wear a back brace to remind you of your back so you don't do something you're not supposed to do.*

BELOW: *It won't prevent most injuries, but a back brace will remind you to keep proper form and not do that thing you shouldn't do.*

38

THE LIFELONG GARDENER

KNEE PAIN

Your knees affect so much about how you move through the world. Be kind to them.

☐ *Use knee pads or knee cushions so you can move easily from sitting to kneeling if you need to. Protect your knees any time you have to kneel in the garden.*

☐ *Install raised beds, which eliminate the need to kneel down.*

☐ *Keep a lightweight chair next to your containers so you can sit instead of kneel.*

☐ *Reduce grades and replace stairs with ramps. Make sure they have firm solid surfaces and handrails.*

HAND STRENGTH

As muscle strength in our hands decreases, opening jars or bags of mulch gets harder, if not impossible. Older gardeners often find their hands don't have the grip they once had.

☐ *Keep a squeeze ball around and squeeze the heck out of it while you watch television.*

☐ *Add cushions to your tool handles.*

☐ *Incorporate adaptive tools with better leverage and improved grips.*

☐ *Investigate children's tools, which are lightweight and can be adapted with extensions.*

☐ *Buy smaller and lighter-weight bags of compost and mulch.*

HAND PAIN

Watch your hands and wrists, which are susceptible to tendinitis or carpal tunnel syndrome. Repeated grip and release movements, like the motions used in pruning, can trigger discomfort. Switch from pruning to less intensely repetitive activities. Arthritis can also cause pain in your hands. When your joints swell, they freeze up and decrease your flexibility, which makes holding tools difficult.

Thankfully there are ways to mitigate pain in your hands:

☐ *Use lightweight tools whenever possible.*

☐ *Add adaptive grips to your current tools or trade them for tools with ergonomics grips.*

☐ *Wear a good quality pair of protective gloves.*

☐ *If dexterity is an issue, avoid tiny seeds and plant with starts or transplants, which are larger and easier to manage.*

☐ *Take regular breaks and switch tasks frequently. Arthritis tends to flare-up after forty-five minutes to an hour of repeated activity.*

☐ *Instead of using a manual pruner or trimmer, try battery powered tools to avoid repetitive movements.*

☐ *Hire help for the heavy lifting, such as planting trees, hauling debris, or any task that causes you pain.*

☐ *Choose easy-to-use gate latches, door handles, and locks.*

☐ *Ask an occupational therapist for exercises to strengthen your grip, keep your pain levels down, and increase your range of motion. All three are critical.*

EYESIGHT

Of our five senses, our vision changes the most as we age. The need for reading glasses is an obvious sign, but other issues, like diminished depth perception can sneak up on you, affecting your idea of how far away or how tall something is—like a step or a curb. In addition to the danger of tripping, compromised depth perception can also be a problem when pruning, which is what happened to me after I had eye surgery. I thought my vision was back to normal . . . and my roses needed to be pruned. So I grabbed my thick gauntlet gloves and my pruners and got to work. However the first cane I cut wasn't a cane at all, but my finger. Thankfully, my gloves protected me.

Here are some ways to help you navigate gardening with compromised vision:

☐ *Wear gloves to protect your hands from plants and from yourself.*

☐ *Use a one-handed pruner for pruning so the other hand is free to feel the plant.*

☐ *For safety on patios and paths, incorporate different colors on the hardscape to mark transitions or to indicate a change in grade.*

☐ *Avoid curved pathways and plan straight paths instead. Mark changes in direction with a change in the texture of the path or plant material.*

☐ *Change the color of your tool handles to make them easy to find.*

☐ *Use other sense markers like wind chimes, water features, and lightly scented plants to help distinguish certain parts of the garden.*

☐ *Utilize vertical gardening to keep things up close, so you and your visitors don't need to bend down.*

☐ *Large flowers in bold red, orange, yellow, and white colors are a pleasure for the visually-impaired.*

☐ *Avoid plants with thorns.*

Keep in Mind

Bold, bright flowers are easy to appreciate if your eyesight is fading. I recently planted blue pansies in my window boxes, and as I walk through my home and see the gorgeous colors, my heart sings.

SKIN

As we get older our skin gets more sensitive to the sun. Older gardeners are generally concerned about too much sun exposure. Sun damage and time also cause our skin to get thinner. Have you ever knocked against something, or caught your hand or forearm on a thorn and gotten tagged with a sore-looking bruise? These are called "senile purpura" (great name, huh?) and are a result of our thinner skin. They don't hurt, thankfully, but they do take forever to go away. I had a cluster of them on my arm for eight weeks after I got tangled up in my climbing roses!

☐ *Wear a hat that is UPF 50 for the best sun protection.*

☐ *Apply a broad-spectrum sunscreen 45 SPF or higher to your hands and arms and re-apply it every few hours.*

☐ *Wear long sleeves and gloves to protect your arms and hands from scrapes and snags.*

Apply and repeat.

TEMPERATURE SENSITIVITY

Older gardeners are more sensitive to weather. We don't tolerate high and low temperatures as well as our younger friends. Hot temperatures, in particular, will sap your strength, making you susceptible to heatstroke and dehydration. During hot summer months, it is critically important to stay hydrated to avoid dehydration. Studies have shown that when you feel thirsty, your ability to regulate heat begins to decline. For seniors, dehydration can deter the body's natural cooling processes even more.

KNOW YOUR LIMITS IN THE HEAT

The Centers for Disease Control and Prevention (CDC) recommends the following gardening tips during the hottest months:

- ☐ If you're outside in hot weather, drink more fluids than you usually do. Make sure to drink *before* dehydration or heat stroke set in.

- ☐ Avoid drinking liquids with alcohol or sugar.

- ☐ Eat healthy foods to get you energized.

- ☐ Schedule all outdoor activities carefully, and pace yourself. Even being out for short periods of time in high temperatures can increase your risk for heat-related illnesses such as extremely high body temperature, headache, rapid pulse, dizziness, nausea, confusion or unconsciousness.

- ☐ Keep cold packs in the freezer so they're ready when you need them for heat relief or to soothe a sore muscle.

- ☐ Take breaks often in shaded areas so your body's thermostat can recover.

45

YOU AND YOUR BODY

Try some of these solutions to mitigate the effects of weather:

☐ *Create shady spots around the garden with comfortable seating and to provide a convenient resting place.*

☐ *Garden early in the morning or late in the day to avoid high temperatures.*

☐ *Wear a hat, gloves, and sunscreen always.*

☐ *Find a favorite water bottle to keep hydrated and prevent heat stroke. Choose one that's insulated to keep your water cold, has a wide-mouth for drinking gulps rather than sips, and is dishwater safe and BPA free.*

☐ *During heat waves, drink water and juices at every meal, and drink fluids throughout the day.*

☐ *Find protection from weather extremes.*

DRESS TO PROTECT

☐ Wearing a wide-brimmed hat is one of the smartest things you can do for yourself, especially if it has a UPF50 rating, which gives the best sun protection. Keep in mind, baseball hats only shield your forehead and maybe your eyes, but they will not protect your face from the sun, so the keyword to remember is wide-brimmed. During the heat of summer, opt for a lightweight hat with a wide-brim and a veil in the back to keep the sun off your neck.

☐ Wear sunglasses or protective eyewear while doing yard work.

☐ Wearing white or light-colored clothing will help you stay cooler. Dark colors absorb the sun's heat and will keep you warm in cool or windy weather. The best colors to garden in are khaki, tan, or gray, because they don't absorb light and heat as quickly as other colors. Avoid bright colors, like bright yellow and blue because they may attract insects.

☐ Wear cotton because it breathes and is cooler in hot weather.

☐ Wear sturdy shoes with a back on the heel, so you won't accidentally walk out of the shoe and fall. Gone are the days of slip-on, slip-off garden clogs.

☐ Gloves protect you from thorns and other threats that can cause cuts or bruises. There are so many different kinds of gloves on the market—find two or three that fit well and will work for the different kinds of gardening chores you

do. Look for gloves that will breathe and be comfortable on hot days.

☐ Protect your arms by wearing long-sleeved shirts, buy yourself sun sleeves from stores like REI, or create your own from socks! All help to keep the sun off your arms when you're in the garden.

☐ Protect yourself from diseases caused by mosquitoes and ticks. Wear long-sleeved shirts, and pants tucked in your socks. You may also want to wear high rubber boots since ticks are usually located close to the ground. At the end of the day, remember to check your clothes and body for ticks.

LEFT: So many choices, so few excuses.

RIGHT: DIY sun sleeves made from tall socks are the height of fashion, and you won't convince me otherwise.

MEMORY

I almost forgot to mention those "senior moments" we all experience. Our memories change as we age. Think about all the funny conversations we have about how lousy our memories have gotten.

. . . When you walk into a room and suddenly
have no clue why you're there.

. . . When the word you're looking for
is on the tip of your tongue, but you cannot
for the life of you remember it.

. . . When you misplace the charger for your leaf blower
not once but three times, and each time you know you
put it in a "safe place" you couldn't forget (ahem, not
speaking from experience or anything).

□ *Keep a log when you fertilize your garden or put a note on your calendar. This way you won't over-fertilize, and your plants won't starve because you forgot to feed them.*

□ *Photograph your garden each year to help you remember what you planted where. Use this method to ensure you don't plant the same crop in the same place the following year.*

□ *Tag your plants. A fellow Garden Writers Association friend, Mary-Kate MacKey, found it best to tag her plants with their names, the year they were planted, and their eventual size.*

□ *Keep a garden journal, garden room by garden room. I record the plants in each space and document the layout on a simple drawing. Do it in pencil in case you make a mistake or end up needing to move plants around.*

□ *Organize plant tags on binder rings for easy reference.*

□ *If you're computer savvy, there are websites that can help with some of these memory techniques. I've heard plantsmap.com is a good place to start.*

GARDENER PROFILE

PAT RANDOLPH

A **SEVENTY-SOMETHING GARDENER**, Pat Randolph is free of any serious physical limitations, but she *has* noticed a few changes in her body of late. For one, she doesn't have the stamina she once had. She has had to accept that she cannot work in her garden for long periods of time without getting tired, so she bites off smaller projects to accomplish in an hour or two and celebrates when each is completed.

Pat's hillside backyard is her greatest challenge. Several years ago, she had the stairs rebuilt and fortified and she added a sturdy handrail. Now the climb is safer, but in order to tend her garden, she needs to step off the stairs and go under the handrail onto the slope, some of which is uneven and often slippery. Knowing this wasn't the safest situation, Pat made an agreement with her partner, Fred, that she wouldn't work the garden on the slope unless he was home.

Pat knows she needs to make changes to her garden to make it safer and ultimately more comfortable to work in. Here are some modifications she's considering:

1 Letting the top part of their garden, which no one ever sees, go natural and see what happens.

2 Looking for opportunities to create places where she can stand safely

and have something to hold on to for balance.

3 Planting more succulents, grasses, and herbs like rosemary that require little or no maintenance.

4 Bringing in a helper once a month to do some of the heavy work. Fred does the sweeping, hedging, and digging holes for Pat, but he's not getting any younger either. A helper would help them both.

I asked Pat if she wouldn't mind sharing her greatest fear about gardening and she had two:

☐ Falling down the hill and breaking something.

☐ Not being able to keep up with her gardening.

One of Pat's favorite tools is a PotLifter, which enables her and Fred to move pots around their patio with great success. (I was relieved to know they don't use the PotLifter when they're on the hill. Whew!)

To help her save energy from switching between kneeling and standing, Pat gardens with a small shovel and a hand rake she can use without getting up. They are short, lightweight, and easy to use.

Pat has sensitive skin on her forearm, so she came up with a super simple solution to keep them protected from the sun as well as thorns and sharp branches. She cut the feet off a pair of tall socks and wears the leg part on her forearms. Once, when she was having sensitivity issues at her elbow, she left on the heel of the sock, which bent conveniently to cover it.

The stairs may be safe, but what happens when you step off them?

Move It or Lose It

Nothing sucks the fun out of gardening faster than pain—and with all the physical changes we go through as we age, pain can feel inevitable. Many gardeners think they are controlling their pain by doing fewer physical activities, but the opposite is true. Being active can delay the functional decline that accompanies aging. As we get older, if we don't get up and move around as much as we can, soon we will not be able to move at all. Any activity is better than being sedentary. As my mom always used to say to my dad, "use it or lose it."

PREVENT FALLS

According to the CDC, falls are the leading cause of injuries in people age sixty-five and older. Falls can happen anywhere, anytime, at any age, but older adults fall more easily and more often.

Most falls experienced by older adults result from three types of risk factors:

Physical risk factors: Changes to your vision, low stamina, low energy levels, and fatigue are common trip-and-fall causes. Arthritis can prevent a gardener from lifting their foot high enough to get onto the side of their raised bed. Medications for conditions like allergies, insomnia, or depression can lower blood pressure and cause dizziness or light-headedness. Make sure to review your

TONI'S TIP

There are so many great ways to get moving! Do something like walking fast or dancing to your favorite music to increase your heart rate for a few minutes and warm up your muscles. What was your favorite dance music when you were in high school or college? Turn up the volume and dance! Need something more? Yoga can increase your flexibility and strength. Tai-chi improves your balance and gait. Check out your local parks and recreation facilities, YMCA, or private health clubs for more ways to supplement your garden activity.

Consult a health care professional prior to attempting any specific stretches.

medications with your doctor or pharmacist, so you're not surprised in the garden.

Physical risk factors can be mitigated by good habits. Posture gets more important as we age, and good posture can help reduce falls. You're better balanced when your body is in proper alignment, and more likely to catch yourself from falling. One of the best ways to avoid falls is to keep your body strong with exercise and to stay active.

Behavioral risk factors: Many older adults don't realize or want to admit their risk of falling has increased. Before starting a chore, consider if it's something safe for you to do.

Consider how you might reduce the risk of a fall. Plan ahead. Ask for help. Organize your garden and tool shed so things are easy to reach.

Environmental risk factors: Ladders are the #1 reason for falls, but branches and tree limbs, hoses, hand tools, containers, and uneven ground and hardscape are also common culprits. Clear clutter to avoid any and all tripping hazards in your garden, tool shed, and garage. And stay off ladders!

STRETCH IT OUT

Stretching before any physical activity, including gardening, can help you prevent pain and injury by warming up your muscles.

To help explain some of the best warm-up stretches for gardeners, I turned to fitness expert Dr. Suki Munsell, who has taught dance, fitness, and biomechanics to students of all ages for more than forty-five years, beginning in 1975 under the guidance of post-modern dance pioneer Anna Halprin.

Relaxed shoulders help with posture and balance.

Dynamic Vitality Exercises for Gardeners by Dr. Suki

This series is designed specifically for gardeners who want to age actively. You will develop greater flexibility, core strength, and balance. You will nurture your sense of well-being, of caring for nature from the inside out. Practice these exercises before gardening to limber up and afterwards to rebalance from your efforts. Most exercises can be done standing; some are designed for sitting. Always start small and respect your range, which changes daily like the weather and the seasons.

BALLOON BREATHING

This exercise expands the chambers of your lungs to absorb more breath energy. It is both energizing and relaxing, and it connects you to nature. With practice, you will notice being able to breathe more fully.

- [ ] Sit comfortably, tall yet relaxed, with both hips evenly balanced on the chair.

- [ ] Place both feet on the ground, widened apart and equally pressing down to support a balanced posture.

- [ ] Start by exhaling fully.

- [ ] Pause, wait for the inhale, then, fill your torso like a balloon—in back, to the sides, and in the front.

- [ ] Sit quietly. Close your eyes and notice all sensations and the flow of life within you.

NOTE: *Use Balloon Breathing for every exercise to maximize your results. Always coordinate full breaths with your movements.*

SHOULDER CIRCLES

This exercise relaxes your shoulders for better posture and balance. With practice, you will notice your shoulders feeling more relaxed.

- [ ] Sit tall as in the first exercise, hips and feet equally weighted, feet widened.

- [ ] Lift your shoulders up.

- [ ] Circle shoulders back, squeeze your shoulder blades together, and widen through your chest.

- [ ] Drop your shoulders, press them down and elongate your neck.

- [ ] Round your shoulders forward and widen through your back.

- [ ] Lift and repeat 3 times.

- [ ] Rest, relax, and feel your results. Imagine your shoulders hanging relaxed like a coat on a hanger.

NECK AND EYE CIRCLES

This exercise relaxes your neck, head and eyes to increase blood flow to your brain and sense organs to improve brain function and balance. With practice, you will notice objects may seem clearer and brighter and smells richer.

- [ ] Sit tall as in the previous exercise, hips and feet equally weighted, feet widened.

- [ ] Lift and lower your chin as if to nod *yes*. Look up and down with your eyes, too.

- [ ] Return to facing forward.

- [ ] Turn your head side to side as if nodding *no*. As you turn your head gently, look behind to your right then your left.

- [ ] Return to facing forward.

- [ ] Tilt your right ear toward you right shoulder, and look up to the left then return to center.

- [ ] Tilt your left ear toward your left shoulder and look up to your right then return to center.

- [ ] Make circles with your chin. Imagine your head like a ball circling gently at the top of your spine.

- [ ] Sit quietly. Close your eyes and notice any sensations and feelings.

FINGER AND FEET FANS, PLUS SELF-MASSAGE

These chair exercises loosen wrists and fingers joints. They increase blood flow and circulation, both vital for decreasing pain from arthritis. The ankle rotations improve flexibility for responsive balance and a sprightlier walk. With practice, you will notice it is easier to hold and use tools.

- [ ] Sit tall as in the previous exercise, hips and feet equally weighted, feet widened.

LEFT: *Loosen your neck to improve brain function and balance.*

RIGHT: *Increase blood flow in hands and feet.*

- [ ] Circle your wrists first in one direction 6–8 times, then in the other direction.

- [ ] Coordinate your breathing to your movements.

- [ ] Repeat the wrist circles as you spread and fan your fingers, first 6–8 times in one direction then the other.

- [ ] Repeat the wrist circles as you add shoulder rotations, first in one direction 6–8 times then the other.

- [ ] Return to center and notice your results.

- [ ] Use one hand to massage the palm and then each finger of the other hand.

- [ ] Twist and pull each of your ten fingers as you mobilize as many joints as possible.

- [ ] Put your palms and fingers together. Separate only the heel of your hands (your elbows will lift up) and stretch your fingers back.

- [ ] Sit quietly. Close your eyes and feel your results.

- [ ] Sit tall as you circle one or both ankles first in one direction 6–8 times, then the other.

- [ ] Spread and fan your toes as much as you can.

- [ ] Sit quietly and notice your results.

ARCH AND CURL

This exercise keeps your spine flexible, the secret to active aging. Spinal exercises also massage your internal organs and circulate the lymphatic fluids so important for immunity. With practice, you will notice that your spine feels more limber when gardening.

- [ ] Sit forward on your chair, feet widened.

- [ ] Sit comfortably, tall yet relaxed, with both hips evenly balanced on the chair.

- [ ] Place both feet on the ground, equally pressing down to support stronger, balanced posture.

- [ ] Place your palms on your thighs with your shoulders relaxed.

- [ ] Exhale and curl your spine forward into a capital C. Relax your shoulders as you elongate.

- [ ] Inhale and return to tall posture.

- [ ] Exhale and arch your spine backward in a capital C. Relax your shoulders as you elongate.

- [ ] Inhale and return to a tall posture.

- [ ] Repeat 6–8 times in each direction comfortably increasing your range.

- [ ] Sit quietly and notice the sensations in your body, the movement within the stillness.

TWIST AND SIGH

This exercise improves spinal rotation so it is easier to twist to either side and to reach high or low. With each exhale, relax your jaw, face, shoulders, and inner organs. With practice, you'll notice it's easier to turn around or reach around behind you.

- [ ] Sit tall as in the previous exercise, hips and feet equally weighted, feet widened.

- [ ] Place both feet on the ground, pressing down equally on each foot for postural support.

- [ ] Reach your right palm over to the outside of your left thigh just above your knee.

- [ ] On an exhale use your hand pressure to help yourself sequentially twist to your left. Begin at your hips, then twist each vertebra of your spine from bottom to top until reaching up to your neck and head. Look as far behind as is comfortable to stretch your eye muscles.

- [ ] Remain twisted and inhale and exhale then return to facing forward.

LEFT: *Keep your spine flexible.*

RIGHT: *Great exercise for fluid spinal rotation.*

- [ ] Inhale and exhale. Sit tall, shoulders relaxed, both hips and both feet equally pressing down.

- [ ] Exhale and repeat to your right. Use your left hand on the outside of your right thigh to help you sequentially twist your spine. Imagine your spine like a towel being twisted and lengthened. Inhale and exhale then release back to center.

- [ ] Repeat the sequence a total of 6–8 times.

- [ ] Sit quietly. Close your eyes and notice any changes.

Hip-hip! Do this exercise for good balance.

HIGH HIP, LOW HIP

This exercise develops independent hip action for good balance. You can do this seated or standing. If standing, keep your spine length-ened as you bend forward at the hips. Position your hands on your thighs just above your bent knees for stable support. With practice, you will notice feeling more stable on your feet.

- [ ] Sit tall as in the previous exercise, hips and feet equally weighted, feet widened.

- [ ] Place both feet on the ground, pressing down equally to support good posture.

- [ ] Place your palms on your thighs with your shoulders relaxed.

- [ ] Lift your right heel off the ground and your right hip off the chair. Lower hip and heel. Coordinate with your breathing.

- [ ] Repeat the exercise on the left, lifting and lowering left heel and hip.

- [ ] Repeat the exercise on both sides 4–6 times.

- [ ] Without lifting or lowering your heels, repeat on both sides. Isolate and strengthen those core muscles you need for High Hip, Low Hip.

- [ ] Sit quietly and notice your results.

LEANING PLANK WITH SHOULDER PUSH-UPS

These exercises build a stronger core from your feet up through your trunk. Your back and shoulders will also strengthen. With practice, you'll notice it's easier to keep your arms up for longer when using tools. It's best to perform this from standing.

☐ Stand tall equally weighted on both feet, shoulders relaxed, full torso breathing.

☐ Face a wall or railing with your feet 1–2 feet away.

☐ Keep your spine straight as you lean forward *from your ankles* into a plank position with your hands against the railing.

☐ Keep your shoulders down and relaxed rather than sliding forward on your ribcage.

☐ Gently pull your belly button toward your backbone and feel your core muscles engage.

☐ Inhale as you hold this position for 6–10 seconds.

☐ Do push-ups by alternately dropping closer to the railing then pushing away. Repeat 6–8 times to build upper back and shoulder strength, and to stretch your calves.

☐ Push away from the railing to return to standing tall. Notice the feelings in your core.

LEANING PLANK INTO LEG STRETCHES

These exercises stretch muscles in your torso and legs. They help balance the front and back of your whole body for better posture. With practice, you'll notice better support and flexibility when reaching to prune. Perform standing only.

☐ Stand tall, equally weighted on both feet, shoulders relaxed, full torso breathing.

☐ Face a wall or railing with your toes 1–2 feet away from it.

☐ Keep your spine straight as you lean forward *from your ankles* into a plank position with your hands against the railing.

☐ Keep your shoulders down and relaxed rather than sliding forward on your ribcage.

☐ Maintain a plank position as you step in closer to the railing with your left foot. Press your back right heel firmly down to stretch your back calf muscle. (Step further back if you need more stretch.) Hold in position for three full breaths.

☐ Arch your back slightly to stretch your front right thigh muscle. Feel a gentle pull on the front from your right knee up to your right hip. Hold in position for three full breaths.

☐ Return to plank position then switch legs.

☐ Step into the railing with your right foot. Press your back left heel. Hold in position for three full breaths.

☐ Arch your back slightly to stretch your front left thigh muscle. Feel a gentle pull on the front from your left knee up to your left hip. Hold in position for three full breaths.

☐ Return to plank position as you step forward with your back foot so your feet are side by side.

☐ Push your body away from the railing and come to standing.

☐ Reach your arms overhead to stretch, then return them to your sides while standing.

☐ Notice the pulsation of life within you and surrounding you.

Use Proper Form

Just as plants pruned in natural forms thrive in gardens, so will you benefit from working with your body, not against. Using proper form reduces stress on your joints, which helps you exert less energy and work longer.

There are some simple steps you can take to make sure that when you work in the garden you're using the correct muscles to do a chore safely and efficiently, so you can be pain free. Here are a couple suggestions:

☐ *Keep your wrists and joints in a straight, neutral position as much as possible. Attach ergonomic grips to your tools to support this alignment.*

☐ *Keep your spine and back straight, in a neutral position—never twisted or rounded. Use your feet to pivot. Keep your center of gravity low. If you find yourself in an awkward position, stop and find another way.*

☐ *For good posture, stand with your feet apart, one foot slightly ahead of the other. Put your weight on the outside of your feet.*

OPPOSITE, FROM LEFT: *Bend with your legs, not with your back.*

Lift with your legs strong.

Carry loads close to your body for balance.

Keep in Mind

An elastic brace for your back, knee, or wrist will not prevent an injury, but it will remind you to think before you twist or do something that might cause re-injury or create pain.

☐ *Bend down by squatting through your knees and hips, rather than at your waist.*

☐ *Lift using your leg muscles, not your back, and lift straight up in one movement. If you want to move something, it may be easier to pull it, push it, or roll it.*

☐ *Carry things close to your body with your elbows tucked in. When you are ready to put them down, bend at the knees and hips.*

☐ *Reach for high objects without twisting your body.*

☐ *Use a stepstool rather than a ladder, which forces you to lean and twist to the side.*

LET'S GET ONE THING (YOUR WRIST) STRAIGHT

When choosing a new garden tool, find one that allows your wrist to be in a straight, non-twisted, or what is called a neutral position. If you have to twist your wrist to use a tool, and you repeat that movement over and over, you can cause yourself unnecessary pain.

ABOVE: *This wrist is stretching tendons and compressing tissues, which will eventually cause pain.*

BELOW: *The best position for your hand and wrist is a neutral, stress-free position.*

Change It Up

Let's face it, gardening requires a great deal of repetitive movement, kneeling, squatting, gripping, stooping, and lifting, all of which can create or add to your existing back pain, knee injuries, and a myriad of other physical issues. Here's a few suggestions to help you switch it up and keep pain at bay:

☐ *Vary your gardening tasks every thirty minutes to avoid doing the same repetitive moments for an extended period of time. If any one movement causes you pain, find other chores that use different muscles, tendons, and ligaments, so no one area is over-worked. Prune for a while, then rake, then transplant or weed. Don't wait for your body to tell you it is time to switch.*

☐ *Instead of bending and stooping, try to work with support at waist level. This might mean using a small garden bench in situations where you'd otherwise be squatting down or bending over.*

☐ *Protect against shoulder and elbow soreness by avoiding excessive twisting and reaching. Make sure your work area is low enough you don't have to raise your hands above your shoulders.*

☐ *Avoid overhead work. This includes repeatedly reaching up high to trim or prune. Use long-handled tools or a sturdy outdoor stepstool to safely reach higher.*

☐ *Use a wagon, cart, or dolly to move heavy objects.*

☐ *Find ways to avoid moving heavy objects entirely. Position a heavy bag of mulch a few steps above a light, plastic tote and let gravity help you pour the contents from the bag to the tote for distribution. You can always buy smaller bags of mulch or compost, though this is more expensive in the long run.*

☐ *Take breaks often. Rest in shaded areas so your body's thermostat has a chance to recover. Stop working if you experience breathlessness or muscle soreness.*

☐ *And finally, listen to your body. Many of us have a twenty year old brain inside a significantly older body that whispers, "It's ok, I'll just do a little bit more, then I'll quit." Don't do it. Don't push yourself if your body is talking to you, telling you to stop.*

It's All in the Timing

I used to garden all weekend—then one Monday morning, I was so sore I could barely get out of bed. Those long sessions in the garden just don't work for me anymore. I'm always asking other gardeners if they've made any changes to how they garden as they've gotten older. Many of their suggestions have helped me and could work for you too:

☐ *Schedule garden chores by dividing up the work into smaller, bite-sized jobs. You don't have to prune your perennials, weed your north forty, and prune all your roses in one day. Do a little bit every day. If it's too much, call for help.*

☐ *Work in early morning and late afternoon to avoid the heat of the day. The hours between 10 a.m. and 4 p.m. (daylight savings time) and 9 a.m. to 3 p.m. (standard time) are the most hazardous for UV exposure outdoors in the continental United States.*

☐ *Take breaks every hour or two. Go in your house and sit down if you need to ice your back for fifteen minutes.*

OPPOSITE: *Vary your tasks, limiting each one to thirty minutes maximum, then do another chore, using another part of the body. Limit the amount of time you spend with your arms above your shoulders. Sit down or kneel down for a while to weed. Take a load off.*

□ *Be opportunistic with your tasks. Plant seeds after a rain or weed when the soil is softer and roots are easier to pull. Transplant shrubs on cloudy days when the digging will be easier on you and the shrubs will suffer less water loss.*

□ *Gardeners with osteoarthritis tend to have more pain as the day goes on, so plan your gardening in the morning hours.*

□ *Gardeners with rheumatoid arthritis often wake up feeling stiff, so save your gardening for the afternoon hours.*

Have you changed when you garden?

We Get by with the Help of Our Friends

If you have balance issues, you know in your gut that should not be getting on a ladder to trim your hedges. It's important to trust that gut reaction, accept what is, and start finding help. If you have family nearby, ask your adult children and grandchildren to do some of the heavy lifting, digging, and other jobs you shouldn't or prefer not to do anymore. If you're delegating chores to a paid helper, be clear about the extent of the job, how long you expect it to take, and what you are willing to pay. Ask them to bring their own ladder.

I know some of you will think hiring help in your garden is giving up, but let's take a moment to look at it from another point of view. Remember earlier when I talked about expecting ease? If that sounds like something you would like to practice, and increasing resilience sounds like a good idea, then hiring help isn't giving up, it's taking control. All you have to do is stand and point. Try it, I think you'll like it.

HOW TO ASK
FOR HELP

Do you need help, but are afraid to ask for it? Start with a gardener friend or someone else you know you can trust. They may be able to refer you to helpers you can try.

Next, practice your call. If it helps you to be more comfortable, write down a couple sentences so you know what to say. For example: "Hello Bill. I have a question for you, but I'm feeling a little uncomfortable about asking. My hedges need trimming and I need to hire someone to handle it for me. Is there any way you could help me find someone?" Practice it. Then try it for real. You will be amazed how often people say yes when you ask for help.

My friend and photographer for this book, Heidi Hornberger, decided she wanted to grow a big veggie garden but knew she didn't have the time nor the energy to do it by herself, so she asked her sister for help. Her sister brought her daughters and they happily planted their first garden together. That was in 2002, and now her sister's daughters and her granddaughter look forward to helping in the garden and harvesting the fruits of their labor as a family.

Three generations gardening together.

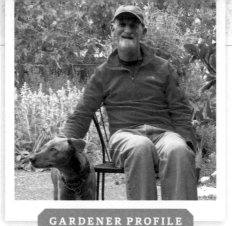

GARDENER PROFILE

MARTY MARCUS

MARTY MARCUS HAD TWO HEART ATTACKS: one in 2011, another in 2013. Ten months later, he suffered a stroke that affected the left side of his body.

In the aftermath, Marty experienced loss of mobility and balance; bending over and reaching up were especially challenging. Beyond that, he struggled with his self-identity and daily reminders of his perceived limitations.

Five years later, Marty's balance is still affected, and he experiences dizziness when he bends over to rake, weed, or plant in his garden. He has tingling in his left arm and can't grip well with that hand, making it challenging to pick up small things. Because he takes blood thinners, he has to be very careful about using knives and pruners, and he leaves tending the roses to his wife, Fran.

Marty no longer uses a ladder and he doesn't prune shrubs taller than he is. Because he's most comfortable gardening standing up, they had four waist-high raised beds built so he wouldn't have to bend over. He avoids gardening in the hottest part of the day and works for shorter periods of time.

He delegates pruning the trees in his backyard orchard to a fellow Master Gardener who is a landscaper, and he hires someone else to maintain the drip irrigation system. Marty doesn't shovel soil, and Fran has taken over the weeding. However, Fran is getting older too, and weeding is growing more challenging. Since they both enjoy gardening, they're considering hiring someone to come in and weed, especially in the spring

Marty's favorite tool is his Fiskars pruner with an ergonomic grip that makes it easy and comfortable to use.

He loves his reversible kneeler seat with attached pockets so he always has his tools close by. He also uses a Worx leaf blower that makes quick work of clearing leaves and debris—it even comes with an attachment to clean out his gutters without getting on a ladder.

Garden Party: Get It Done, then Have Fun!

There's no better way to feel young than to hang around with other fun-loving, down to earth gardeners for an afternoon. Better yet, start taking turns having garden work parties to help each other out.

Spring is a perfect time for to make this happen, because there is so much to do to get your garden ready—or maybe you could use help putting your garden to bed in the fall. Whatever needs to be done, I can guarantee it will be more fun if you do it with other people.

The year I had eye surgery and nearly cut off my finger trying to prune my roses, I knew I needed help. So I called up some friends and explained my dilemma, promising if they came over to help, when we finished working in the garden, I would feed them a fabulous lunch. I had three goals: garden together, eat great food, and laugh a lot. We accomplished all three!

Ten o'clock Saturday morning, we got started. After surveying my roses, which desperately needed to be de-leafed and pruned, a few of my friends started in on those, while others planted some ground-cover with me (I was resolved to avoid sharp tools until my vision returned to normal). After the work, I served a lovely lunch, catered by my husband Tim, of three different salads made with lettuces from our garden, crusty Italian bread, olives, homemade basil lavender lemonade, and finally a homemade raspberry sorbet.

It was a riot. We talked about everything under the sun related to gardening. One woman talked about how happy she was that she'd planted the perennial basil, Pesto Perpetuo, which had over-wintered beautifully. Another shared her new favorite pruner that fit her hand so well she couldn't live without it.

We eventually got around to discussing the funny side of the aging process. My friend Janet

There is nothing more fun than working, laughing, and breaking bread together.

laughed hysterically telling us how many trips she had to make back into the house that morning because she couldn't remember everything she needed to bring. We each had a funny story to share about "the joys of aging."

If you'd like to throw your own garden-work party or organize one for a friend in need, write down a list of projects that need to be done and prioritize them. Put together an invite list and decide what you'll serve for lunch as a thank you—it's always an extra special touch to serve something fresh from your garden that day. Be realistic how

GARDEN PARTY CHECKLIST

This is just a sampling of possible tasks you can do at your Garden Party!

- ☐ Spring garden clean-up
- ☐ Harvest party in the fall
- ☐ Deadheading and pruning
- ☐ Making compost tea

- ☐ Build a raised bed and plant it
- ☐ Create a square foot garden & plant it
- ☐ Plant herbs and medicinal gardens

- ☐ Build a chicken coop
- ☐ Plant bulbs, groundcover, or a tree
- ☐ Weeding
- ☐ Spread compost and mulch

much you can get done in a couple hours, but think up a couple extra tasks in case your helpers finish early. Then share a feast together. It can be as elegant or laid back as you want. If you have a gardener friend who you know is struggling, volunteering to plan and spearhead a garden party for them is a lovely way to show support.

Join a Community Garden

You know gardeners. We're an easy bunch to talk to. We love to share our successes and failures as well as our seeds, cuttings, and pups. Having your own plot at a community garden is one of the fastest ways to get to know new people and grow your community at the same time.

Growing food, growing your community. That's what it's all about!

OPPOSITE:
It's always fun working together and helping our community at the same time.

In most cities and towns, it doesn't cost very much to rent a raised bed of your own. It is fun to experiment growing different kinds of plants, and a joy to share the fruits of your labor with your fellow gardeners, family, and friends. Growing your own vegetables is not only a great way to save money at the grocery store, but it is also a fun lesson in "where food comes from" for any grandkids or other children in your life. Chances are you'll also be inspired by your neighbors—many community gardeners grow food for the local food bank.

If you are interested in getting a plot, stop by your local community garden and ask about how participation works. Don't wait to inquire, as many community gardens have a wait-list.

When you are deciding what to plant in your plot, consider planting *lots* of leafy green vegetables. Studies have shown that people who eat more dark leafy greens have slower cognitive decline with age than those who eat the standard American diet.

Become a Master Gardener

Are you interested in learning more about gardening? Do you like working with people? Do you enjoy volunteering?

If so, contact your county cooperative extension office to find out about your local Master Gardener program. Once you complete the course, your only obligation is to share your knowledge with your community. The bonus comes because you get to meet hundreds of like-minded people and gain friends for life.

The procedures for becoming a Master Gardener differ from state to state. Here in California, the University of California Master Gardener Program extends research-based information about home horticulture, pest management, and sustainable landscape practices to the residents of California.

We attend a sixteen-week (one day a week) training program. Once graduated, UC Master Gardeners are required to volunteer fifty hours the first year and twenty-five hours each subsequent year. We must complete a minimum of twelve hours of continuing education per year, starting our second year, so we're always learning new things.

WHY BECOME A MASTER GARDENER?

My life changed for the better when I became a Master Gardener. I used to wonder why I seldom saw people I knew when I was out in my community. That question ended in 2011 when I graduated from the program—our small county has 350 Master Gardeners. Now I see someone I know at most functions, especially at garden tours and public seminars. I can't always remember their names, but that's another story.

Pat Randolph became a Master Gardener a year after retiring because she liked being active and wanted to make a contribution. Having worked in a medical setting, she liked the idea of learning research-based gardening and she wanted to give back to her little corner of the world. I asked Pat how being a Master Gardener changed her life; her answer tells the whole story. "My life is rich with many friends I would not have if I were not a Master Gardener."

After Marty Marcus had a stroke, his daughter encouraged him to volunteer. He decided to become a Master Gardener because he wanted something purposeful to do with his life. He likes learning and sharing his knowledge with his community. Marty's greatest fear is not being able to continue volunteering due to physical limitations.

Joe Jennings thought he knew something about gardening, having grown up gardening with his mother in Seattle. But one year, he had a horrible time growing tomatoes, and a friend of his wife suggested he go through the Master Gardener program. He liked the idea because their main goal was to share research-based information with a community of home gardeners. After becoming a member, Joe volunteered for the tomato market, and for the last several years, he's given public seminars on how to grow great vegetables and be successful growing tomatoes.

Working in the garden gives me something beyond the enjoyment of the senses. It gives me a profound feeling of inner peace.

RUTH STOUT

OPPOSITE: *What plants do you love? There's a club for that.*

Join a Garden Club

Garden clubs are another great way of meeting new people while learning new information on aspects of gardening you love. There are clubs for roses, irises, begonias, flower arrangers, heirloom flowers, ikebana, fuchsia, geraniums, cactus, succulents, chrysanthemums—you name a flower, there's a club full of members who are passionate about it.

Most garden clubs offer a wide range of educational programs, and bring in speakers on the latest gardening techniques, floral design, conservation, and environmental issues. I've heard many go on fun field trips and have plant sales. In addition, garden clubs develop and participate in a variety of local, state, regional, and national projects.

If you love to garden or just being in gardens, and you're interested in learning more, start making inquiries and visit a meeting of your local garden club. Novices are always welcome.

YOUR
GARDEN

Passion is the bridge that takes you from pain to change.

FRIDA KAHLO

Re-Envision Your Garden
for Ultimate Comfort and Safety

If you love to garden, and you want to continue gardening with gusto, but you know in your heart you need to make some changes, where do you start?

Start where you are. Start with the task or chore that bothers you the most and then you can determine how your garden needs to change to make that job easier on your body.

Find your favorite pen or pencil, a yellow pad, or a garden journal. Pour yourself a cup of coffee or tea, a glass of wine or a cocktail. Go out to your garden, sit in each area, and take a good hard look at everything with your new adaptive-gardening eyes.

What is not working for you? Move from one end of your garden to another and create a new plan as you get ideas. Remember, the more thoughtful your modifications now, the less you'll have to worry later.

Plan your garden on paper.
Mistakes made on paper won't cost you
much in either time or money.

ELSA BAKALAR

Here is a short exercise to get you going:

1 Write down all the wonderful moments you experienced in your garden.

2 In order of most painful to least, write down things you can no longer do without pain or discomfort. Be honest with yourself.

3 Think about what chores you can delete. Make a list of people you can ask for help. Make a list of people who can recommend helpers for hire.

What would you change if you had all the time, money and energy you needed? Go area by area and identify potential changes so you can garden for life in complete comfort. Then of course, consider your budget and assemble a plan to get estimates so you can see what is doable and affordable.

TONI'S TIP

I created an adaptive gardening plan as a handout for whenever I'm teaching or speaking. You will find it at the back of this book. You can also print a copy from my website, *tonigattone.com*.

TEN IMPORTANT TRAITS
FOR A GARDEN OF EASE

1 Safe. How can you change your garden to increase your safety when you're working? Clear away all clutter and any potential tripping hazards. Let go of any tools that are rusted or not safe or easy to use anymore.

2 Comfortable. What modifications would you make to increase your level of comfort in your garden? Do you have seating in the shade? How about chairs next to your raised beds and containers?

3 Fully Accessible. Are all areas of your garden completely accessible or do you have stairs to deal with? Are the trees in your orchard pruned low enough you can harvest without using a ladder?

4 Simple. Less is more, folks, especially in a garden. Fewer tools with more functionality. Fewer plants and more water-wise ones, especially flowering shrubs. Give up the idea of bringing home every new plant you see in the nursery.

5 Sustainable. Whatever changes you make should include your garden's long-term sustainability, which reduces its maintenance needs. Build soil with compost and mulch. Avoid pesticides and herbicides. Be organic and water smart. Use integrated pest management. Create wildlife habitat.

6 Saves You Time. Time is more precious than ever these days. Identify the work that takes you forever to do and hire someone else to do them—they'll do it more efficiently in a lot less time.

7 Saves You Money. Put your money towards getting help where and when you need it, rather than buying more plants to take care of. Grow your collection of colorful, re-purposed containers at garage sales.

8 Saves You Energy. Use a tool sharpener when you first grab your pruners. Sharp blades will make less work of any plant you want to prune.

9 Saves Space. If you decide to give up tending the far corners of your garden, you'll have to fit more of what you love into closer, more accessible spaces. Look

for plants that do double duty or have multiple varieties on one tree. The same goes for your storage shed. You shouldn't have to wrestle with mountains of tools. Find tools that do double duty with multi-functions and tools that fold up for the least amount of storage space.

10 Brings You Joy. Isn't this what gardening is all about? When you're surrounded by plants and flowers that make your heart sing, and you're growing your own veggies and herbs, you'll get the feeling you have everything you need.

OPPOSITE LEFT:
*Bring those beds
up rather than
bend down.*

OPPOSITE RIGHT:
*I love this Black
Jack fig; it only
grows to 8 feet.*

Ease of Access

The #1 goal in re-envisioning your garden is to create an easy-care garden that is kinder to your body.

SMART IDEAS FOR GARDEN ACCESSIBILITY:

☐ *Arrange garden beds near the house and near a driveway if possible, to decrease the distance you and your helpers will have to carry soil and plants.*

☐ *Replace stairs with a sloping curving path for a smooth transition from one level to the next.*

☐ *Texture all hardscape surfaces with a non-slip coating that gives a strong grip underfoot.*

☐ *Make hardscape and railings contrasting colors to enable those with low vision to more easily see the edges of the garden. This will also mark a clear path to and from the door or exit.*

☐ *Remove your lawn, or at least the majority of it, and replace it with low-maintenance and low-water native plants and paved paths.*

☐ *Create multiple places for seating in the garden, particularly next to containers and raised beds and in the shade.*

☐ *Restrict the depth of your garden beds and raised beds to a maximum of 3 to 4 feet deep and use long-reach tools to help you tend them easily.*

☐ *If you have back issues, incorporate containers, raised beds, and vertical garden opportunities, so you can stand up to garden.*

☐ *Prune fruit trees to an easy-to-reach height for maintenance and harvesting, so you don't have to get on a ladder.*

SMART IDEAS FOR TOOLS AND TOOL SHEDS:

☐ *Save time and energy not having to double back for necessary tools. Keep your garden tools within easy reach by having a tool tote bag with you at all times. Don't forget your tool sharpener!*

☐ *Place inexpensive rural mailboxes in various parts of your garden and keep them stocked with your most-used garden tools for quick access.*

☐ *Tool shed doors should be 48 inches wide to accommodate wheelchairs.*

☐ *Use a wheelbarrow or dolly—or hire help—to carry heavy loads.*

☐ *If your debris can has wheels, use them. As my gardening friend Karen Turcotte preaches: bring the can to the job rather than schlepping debris to the can. Alternatively, put debris into a small, portable rubber tote. Limiting the size of your container will keep you from trying to carry too heavy a load.*

A TO-DO LIST FOR ADAPTING YOUR GARDEN:

☐ Assess your limitations and your needs, both physically and financially.

☐ Determine changes you want to make in terms of priority.

☐ Design and plan changes including raised beds, containers, paths, etc.

☐ Check with your local resources and online to get advice.

☐ Decide how much help you need.

☐ Ask friends and fellow gardeners for recommendations for garden helpers, garden maintenance companies and landscape designers, whatever you determine you need to get it done.

OPPOSITE: *You have many options for replacing your lawn, from functional hardscape like this to easy-to-maintain dry gardens.*

Rethink Your Lawn

Grass lawns became the ideal for suburban homes after World War II, but times have changed. More and more homeowners are reducing the size of their lawns or completely replacing them with patios, flowerbeds, raised beds, and even artificial turf for three good reasons:

☐ *It takes a lot of work, as well as precious time and energy to maintain an expanse of lawn and all the necessary watering, mowing, trimming, weeding, fertilizing, raking, and aerating.*

☐ *Lawns are expensive because they use a lot of water, and water prices continue to go up. In contrast, an efficient drip irrigation*

system costs pennies on the dollar. Replacing your lawn with low-water alternatives can put money back into your wallet because in many cities, homeowners can get rebates from their water districts. Check it out!

☐ *Pesticides and fertilizers used to make lawns beautiful run off into our streams and water sources and can have adverse effects on people and animals who may drink from them or eat the fish and other creatures who live in them.*

In recent years, the idea of creating a front yard farm has gained in popularity, allowing homeowners to grow their own herbs, fruits, and vegetables, which enables them to be more self-sufficient and sustainable.

Downsizing

Look around your garden. Are there areas you seldom walk through, that most people don't see, that you could let naturalize? One happy gardener told me, when she downsized by not cultivating every square inch of her garden as she always had, gardening became fun again because all she had to take care of were the most visible areas: in front of her house and in the back where she entertains. Life became easier and simplified.

Many gardeners want acres of land to grow everything they want to grow. Good enough, but the dream of gathering endless bouquets of cut flowers or medicinal herbs can become problematic if physical

SMALL SPACE, SMALL PLANTS

Small gardens force you to minimize your consumption and maximize your small spaces by growing dwarf or semi dwarf plants. In our small yard, I love plants that do their thing without taking up a lot of room.

LEFT: *You can get dwarf citrus of all kinds that will give you a great crop of limes or lemons without demanding the space a standard size tree will take.*

RIGHT: *One of my all-time favorite space-saving plants is an espaliered apple tree with six different kinds of apples! Mine is only 6 feet wide and 3 feet high by 12 inches deep, taking up little space but giving so much reward.*

issues begin. This can be the moment when gardeners must
ask themselves:

☐ *How much of a cultivated garden do I really need?*

☐ *How much can I realistically maintain and harvest?*

☐ *Which are my absolute favorite plants?*

☐ *What vegetables, fruit, herbs, and salad greens do I most like to eat?*

☐ *What volume of produce can I consume or preserve over the winter?*

By reducing the size of your gardens, you automatically reduce
the amount of time and energy it takes to keep it looking beautiful.
Downsizing can be challenging in the beginning, but when you
get used to gardening in smaller spaces, you will grow to love "less
is more."

SPACE SAVERS

Over the years, I'd come to think of adaptive gardening as a way to
save gardeners three key elements: time, money, and above all energy.
Recently, I realized it also saves space.

Space is always an issue, but when you downsize, it forces you to
consider every inch, not only in your garden itself but also where you
store your garden tools. Multi-functional, fold up, or collapsible tools
can help you make the most of small spaces. My favorite debris bin
is made of non-tear polyethylene lined with wire, so it weighs absolutely nothing, but sits up and stays open when in use and folds away
flat for storage.

It's funny how things multiply in our toolsheds over the years. I'm
not sure why I had three rakes when I really only need one. I found

an expandable rake that makes it easy to do all the raking jobs in my garden. It also has a telescopic handle so it's easy to hang up off the floor. As we clear away the clutter from our gardens, garages and toolsheds, we should only keep the pots, fertilizers, and tools we know we're going to need. If certain pots or accessories speak to your heart, keep them. If not, give them away to a neighbor, donate them to a local school or charity, or sell them at a home consignment store.

Enclose Your Yard

As we age, we strive to make life easier. I have a friend who lives on several acres and designed her gardens to attract birds, butterflies, and bees. In the last few years, more critters and animals, specifically deer, have discovered her gardens and she's had to replace many plants, costing her time, energy, and money. For her, the answer was to install a fence, both above and below ground, to protect her garden. If you're on a fixed income, a fence is a good investment, because you won't have to continually replace damaged plants.

How about your garden? Would you feel more secure if your back yard was fenced in? Do you have critters or deer in your neighborhood?

When we moved into our home, we removed the gate thinking it would make our entrance more welcoming. In doing so, we welcomed a family of deer who proceeded to devour the rose bushes in our front yard.

In our suburban neighborhood, the deer walk down the middle of the street like they own it. As beautiful as they are to look at, deer will eat anything, even if it's on the list of plants deer will not eat. As I was informed in my Master Gardener class, the deer didn't get that same list!

Here are few types of fence to consider:

TONI'S TIP

Be sure to add secure latches that are easy for you to open and close, especially if you have arthritis or decreased muscle strength in your hands.

1 A 6- to 8-foot fence will prevent those lovely but destructive deer from jumping over for lunch. Be sure to make your fences close to the ground so the deer cannot go under them.

2 If you're besieged with gophers and moles that tunnel their way in, you'll need to add a 2- to 3-foot deep trench so the fence goes below ground too. Line the garden side with wire mesh.

3 To keep raccoons and opossums out, the fence can be as low as 4 feet but you'll need to curve the wire mesh on the bottom to create a 2-foot apron.

4 Consider a solid fence to provide a visual block, which keeps animals from seeing the tempting, tasty morsels you're growing.

5 Vinyl, wrought iron, bamboo and aluminum fences are all low-maintenance and require no hard work or refinishing, like wood does.

The Hard Truth about Hardscape

While most gardeners focus on the plants in their garden, it's the non-living, man-made hardscape elements that are most important in a well-thought-out adapted garden—mainly because they are the most expensive aspect to change. Uneven paths can be a tripping hazard, and gaps between flagstones or other surfaces can catch heels or canes, causing falls. If you use a walker or wheelchair or have friends that do, your utmost concern must be to ensure it's easy and safe to negotiate through all parts of your garden.

Take pictures of what areas need to be changed, and photograph hardscapes you like in your neighborhood. Consult with professionals. Check out landscape books at the library. Ask your gardener friends. With some careful planning, you can make the necessary changes you'll appreciate every day. Above all, as you do your research, keep in mind which materials will give you easy-care upkeep, and be sure to consider what will be needed for on-going cleaning, sealing or repairing.

LEFT: *Flagstone with gravel in the gaps was not safe and had to go.*

RIGHT: *New hardscape with smart transitions.*

RECONSIDER SURFACE MATERIALS

The best solid surface solutions are concrete, flagstones, or pavers.

POURED CONCRETE patios and paths are low maintenance and less expensive to have installed than other materials. They don't have joints or spaces for shoe heels to get stuck or for weeds to grow through. They can be tinted with stains for color or stamped with patterns to add texture. However, concrete is prone to cracks—they say cracking is a feature of concrete, not a flaw. Concrete surfaces are difficult to repair and require sealing every two to three years.

FLAGSTONE can give a garden a nice informal look that is popular with many gardeners. If your flagstone is still lying flat, in good shape, and the seams or joints are narrow enough a cane can't get stuck, you are fortunate. Many flagstone surfaces develop gaps that are wide and deep—dangerous tripping hazards that should be your #1 goal to eliminate.

PAVERS are blocks of stone used to create patios and paths in a vast array of colors, shapes and patterns. Interlocking pavers won't crack—they lock horizontally to resist side to side shifting, and vertically to keep them from moving up or down. They are easy to repair and easy to expand. They're also the most expensive option initially—they'll typically cost you 10–15 percent more to install than concrete. However, durable pavers are three to four times stronger than concrete and carry a longer warranty.

FLAGSTONE FILLING

If you are having flagstone installed, you are wise to have it cemented in, which will eliminate the dreaded gaps between the stones. If you already have flagstone installed, you'll need to fill in the gaps. The five most commonly used materials to fill in flagstone gaps are:

JOE JENNINGS

WHEN JOE JENNINGS AND HIS WIFE moved into their 1926 California bungalow, they had a mixture of original concrete on the sidewalk, flagstone and gravel paths on the back patio, and a driveway made of permeable concrete pavers and decomposed granite. The key motivators for replacing their hardscape were:

1 Establish a unifying aesthetic that allowed them to replace four different hardscape approaches from the past.

2 Remove tripping and safety hazards.

3 Improve the flow, usability, and ease of access to the entire front, side, and back yards.

Joe and his wife chose 2-inch thick Bluestone pavers for the sidewalk and patios, blue-tinted concrete interlocking pavers for the driveway, and deconstructed granite gravel pathways for the vegetable garden side yard. Particular attention was paid to transitions between walkways and patios and the garden areas. Tripping hazards and uneven surfaces were removed. They installed pathway lighting to improve nighttime use and new stairway handrails to reduce the risk of falling. To improve access and reduce maintenance of the vegetable garden, they relied on galvanized horse troughs (2 feet high × 8 feet long × 3 feet wide).

Here are the key learning points for gardeners with hardscape issues:

1 Upgrading hardscape and lighting is a one-time expense that needs to solve aesthetic, safety, and access problems, not create them. Don't settle for anything less than aesthetically pleasing, safe, and accessible designs.

2 Focus on transitions from garden to paths and sidewalks, and between patios and paths, and eliminate tripping hazards and uneven surfaces. Many designers like raised transitions, bor-

ders, and steps, but you need to insist on smooth transitions if you want to be safe.

3 Surfaces matter: smooth, slick-when-wet surfaces are dangerous. Find surfaces that have year-round use regardless of the weather in your area.

4 Drainage is important and should be part of planning and building any hardscape. Water should drain away from the house and off of sidewalks, paths, and patios. Test new surfaces after construction by flooding them and watching for any puddles that form. Have the contractor fix these before you make your final payment.

ABOVE LEFT:
Permeable driveway with DG was a tripping hazard.

ABOVE RIGHT:
Interlocking pavers are perfect for driveways.

OPPOSITE:
The change in this backyard hardscape made a huge difference.

1 Groundcovers. They're beautiful and quite effective, as long as your area doesn't suffer from the occasional drought, which will cause them to dry up and create more gaps.

2 Decomposed Granite, known as DG, looks great and has many advantages, but what a lot of people don't tell you is that you will need to make additional applications over time because it blows away. It can also be difficult for wheelchair users because the small stones can get stuck in the wheels. They can also get stuck in the treads on the bottom of shoes. I have a friend whose housewarming party ended on a sad note when she realized her guests had unknowingly brought in DG on their shoes, and her brand new cherry wood floors were badly scratched.

3 Artificial turf can work really well and is inexpensive because all you need are scraps to fill in the gaps and it looks great for a long time with no replacement.

4   Gravel, river rocks, and wood chips are my last choice, simply
    because they are always loose and can be an accident waiting to
    happen for anyone with balance issues. They can be a challenge
    for wheelchairs too. Wood chips, in particular, lack the firmness
    and traction needed by gardeners with canes, crutches, walkers,
    and wheelchairs.

Our Hardscape Challenge

We love our garden. It's tiny but eclectic, filled with an array of fun
and functional garden art and gorgeous containers we have collected
over the years. We grow a large variety of succulents, perennials,
flowering shrubs, colorful annuals, an abundant lettuce garden, one
raised bed, and a square-foot garden that should be raised. However,
as soon as you enter the garden, you will see the challenge we have
with our hardscape paths.

Our front pavers are nice and level, but in the back, deep gaps between stones and tall greenery make for an accident waiting to happen.

In the early eighties, we experienced several bad drought years, so when we bought our home in 1985, we knew we had to learn how to be water efficient. Though it seemed like every garden design magazine featured a lawn-less, water-resistant garden with beautiful curving flagstone paths, we weren't quite ready to give up our lawn.

In the summer of 2000, we decided to take the plunge. We removed the grass and my husband happily gave away our lawn-mower. We planted Japanese Maples trees, shrubs, perennials, bulbs, and herbs. Of course, we installed a curving flagstone path inter-spersed with wooly thyme groundcover.

It looked beautiful and it was easy to maintain—until another bad drought hit. The groundcover dried up and we were left with gaps between the stones. Every day, I looked at the paths wondering what we would do if one of us needed a walker or a wheelchair. With those gaps, we'd be challenged to walk through the garden, let alone work in it, without the risk of falling.

Looking at our hardscape through adaptive gardening eyes, we started to see the problems. What's a gardener to do when their hardscape is a safety hazard?

Stairs, Handrails, and Ramps, Oh My!

I once did an adaptive gardening consultation with a gardener who had to climb down twelve stairs to reach her ultra-sunny veggie garden. To make matters worse, she needed knee-replacement surgery. She loved to garden and couldn't imagine life without growing kale, beets, salad greens, herbs, and tomatoes all summer long.

Unsure of the best solution, she decided to take the time she'd be recuperating from knee surgery to answer these two insightful and clarifying questions:

1 Should I replace my stairs and have a ramp installed? If so, where would it go and how much would it cost?

2 Do I sell this house and move to a smaller home with a garden on one level, so that I can garden till I drop?

This is a real problem that many of us may have to face. My client ended up selling her home because after getting several estimates, she found out there wasn't enough room to have a ramp installed.

Be careful only to carry lightweight items down stairs so you don't lose your balance.

LEFT: *Sturdy and strong makes all the difference.*

RIGHT: *Just the right grade and perfect width, with room to turn a wheelchair, this ramp is well built.*

THE SKINNY ON STAIRS

☐ *Stairs preclude wheelchair access and they are, at best, difficult to use with walkers because standard steps are not deep enough.*

☐ *Transform stairs into wide, curving, gently sloping paths.*

☐ *If you must keep them, fortify your stairs to make them safe and sturdy.*

HANDRAILS ARE HANDY

☐ *ADA guidelines require 42-inch-high handrails for ramps and stairs that are higher than 30 inches from the finish grade.*

☐ *Installing sturdy and attractive handrails on ramps and other strategic points throughout the garden will greatly increase safety.*

☐ *The proper size for such a railing is 1 ¼ to 1 ½ inches in diameter.*

RAMPS

☐ *If you have the room, replace stairs with ramps.*

☐ *Ramps consume more room than stairs, so it important to consult with a professional for installation.*

☐ *Switchbacks, curves, and bends in the ramps need to accommodate wheelchair turns.*

☐ *The maximum wheelchair ramp slope ratio is 1:12, which means 1 foot of fall for every 12 linear feet of ramp and it should not exceed 5 percent rise in elevation.*

☐ *Ramp materials need to have a non-slip, textured surface. Concrete or wood flooring are a better choice than brick or stone, because those can become un-level.*

Without Water, Fuhgeddaboudit!

Installing a drip irrigation system benefits both your plants and the planet. Delivery systems like hoses and overhead sprinklers waste water—it evaporates in the air and runs off hard surfaces. A drip irrigation system is much more precise and water efficient. Getting your drip system on a timer pays for itself three ways: it saves you time, money, and above all, energy. This is one of those JUST DO ITs. Do it once, and your watering needs immediately become faster, easier, and cheaper.

ENERGY FIRST:

☐ *You don't have to carry around a hose or watering can. Command the water with the press of a button or two.*

☐ *Bye bye, stress. You can go on vacation and not worry if the girl down the street remembered to water for you.*

MONEY:

☐ *Your water bill will go down because you're using water more efficiently, especially if you water in the morning, the coolest part of the day.*

☐ *Your plants will be happier when they receive regular watering aimed directly at their roots, and therefore they'll live longer, and you won't have to replace them.*

☐ *Some municipal water districts offer rebates when you install a drip irrigation system.*

TIME:

☐ *When you set the timer, you are immediately relieved of watering duties and are free to do other things.*

LEFT: *Drip emitters deliver water straight to a plant's roots.*

RIGHT: *Installation can be intimidating and make you feel like you need an engineering degree. Don't be afraid to ask for help!*

> **TONI'S TIP**
>
> If walking into a drip irrigation store makes you break out in hives like it does me, hire someone to do the installation for you and keep their number handy in case you need your system re-tuned in the future. Ask gardener friends for a recommendation or ask at the drip irrigation store (Then get out as fast as you can!).

Sustainability

Seeking to create a sustainable garden makes perfect sense as we age—it means less labor for you and it leaves something positive for the next generation.

Below is a checklist of things you can do to make your garden more sustainable:

☐ *Go organic. Avoid using pesticides, herbicides, and inorganic fertilizers that pollute our soil and water. If you must use chemicals, chose the least toxic options.*

☐ *Utilize IPM. Check your local county extension department to find the Integrated Pest Management website. You can use it to solve pest problems while minimizing risks to people and the environment.*

☐ *Conserve water. Use a diversity of water-wise plants to keep your water usage down. Water efficiently and deeply with drip irrigation. Use rain barrels to collect runoff and swales to replenish ground water.*

☐ *Compost. Build your soil by using compost as a top dressing once or twice a year. Start a worm bin and feed the worms your kitchen waste; worm castings make a wonderful fertilizer. A good rule of thumb when you're planting is to use 50 percent native soil with 50 percent fresh compost.*

☐ *Mulch. Mulching is such a great thing to do because it signals the end of spring weeding and planting, and it finishes off your garden. When organic mulch is applied two or four inches deep around your plants, the mulch will block out the sun and reduce your weeding. It helps maintain moisture in the ground, will keep the soil tempera- ture even, and provides food for plants.*

☐ *Create wildlife habitat. Replace your lawn with native plants to attract pollinators. We like to plant milkweed, for example, to keep our monarch butterflies coming back. Add bird feeders, and supply water with birdbaths, ponds, and fountains.*

☐ *Choose the right plants. Select native plants that are adapted to your soil and your local climate—these will require less work on your part to stay happy.*

Right Plant, Right Place

One of the many light bulbs that went off in my head when I became a Master Gardener was the concept of *right plant, right place.* When I began to speak and write about adaptive gardening, I knew I needed to include it. After all, we strive to save time, money, and energy, right? Using the concept of *right plant, right place* is a huge factor for lowering maintenance because if you choose the right plant and put it in the right place, you won't have to move it or replace it if is unhappy.

Here are some things to consider and steps to take as you live by the *right plant, right place* mantra:

☐ *A good rule of thumb is to know how big a plant will be in three years. Many of us have made the mistake of falling in love with a plant and putting it in the garden, only to watch it grow past its expected size and start bullying surrounding plants, or simply reach the limits of its space and start to look unhappy. You'll know it's time to transplant these behemoths to another part of your garden or to say good-bye to them.*

☐ *Progressively replace plants that require more water and more care, with those that require less. Replace perennials, which need more maintenance, with low maintenance, long blooming flowering shrubs. Choose easy to grow plants that tolerate frost or high temperatures, are disease free, and don't require a lot of maintenance.*

☐ *Start a collection of easy-to-care-for succulents. They will make pups (baby plants!), and your collection will grow from there.*

☐ *If you have a certain plant you absolutely love, but it doesn't look as good as it once did, give it a good pruning and see how it responds. If it still looks unhappy, if it's tired or leggy or has outgrown its space, it may be time to replace it.*

☐ *Look for pest and disease resistant plants that don't require frequent pruning to look their best.*

☐ *If you love roses, great! Go for it! But recognize when you're ready to surrender. Roses in my garden get black spot pretty bad, and last year I had to de-leaf and spray horticultural oil three times over the spring and summer to get rid of the disease. For the first time as a gardener, I'm considering replacing some of my roses, which will be hard to do because I fell in love with gardening in my grandfather's rose garden. But three times, really? I don't want that much work!*

☐ *Buy plants in the smallest pot possible because this is how they grow: the first year they sleep, the second year they creep, and the third year they leap!*

☐ *Embrace hydrozoning and other forms of strategic grouping. Hydrozoning means grouping together plants with similar water, soil, and sun-exposure needs. If the plants you're putting in are designed to attract pollinators, it's a good idea to plant at least three of a particular species together, so pollinators can see the flowers and "tell their friends" there are enough to make it worth a trip!*

☐ *Gardening is all about trial and error, about hanging on and letting go. At a certain stage, the gardener must look at every plant and ask the hard questions:*

  ☐ *Do I have the time and energy to give this plant what it needs?*

  ☐ *If not, do I love it enough to give it what it needs?*

  ☐ *Should I give it away or toss it?*

IT'S OKAY TO MAKE MISTAKES

It broke my heart to see my beloved fig tree being carried out of my garden. I had made the ultimate gardening mistake: I did *not* pay attention to the concept of right plant, right place when I purchased my Black Mission fig tree.

It was the right plant. My husband and I fell in love with figs in Italy and we wanted to grow our own. We found a Black Mission fig tree at a local nursery and happily planted it near our front gate. It turned out to be not exactly the right place. In fact, it was definitely the wrong

place. Our gorgeous fig wanted to be 25 feet wide, and without pruning, it could grow to be 40 feet wide. Our front yard is 15 feet at its widest point.

One of my dearest gardening friends, Karen Turcotte, came over shortly after the fig was planted. She didn't waste a minute pointing out my error, and she couldn't understand why we hadn't bought a dwarf or even an ultra-dwarf fig. Guilty as charged. I swore I would prune really, really well every winter and I would keep the Black Mission to a manageable height.

Last winter I pruned it to five feet high—that growing season, it doubled in size. In my heart of hearts, I knew my beloved fig had to go; she would never be happy where we'd planted her. Thankfully, I found a local landscaper with a client who was starting an orchard.

I watched while they dug her up. I was sad to see her go, but I was happy she was going to a good home—to an orchard where she could spread her limbs and be all she was meant to be, an exceptional, very large, Black Mission fig tree. Ciao, Bella!

Lesson learned.

BELOW: *The Black Mission fig squeezed into our tiny yard.*

OPPOSITE: *Our yard is no longer in danger of being taken over by a giant fig tree.*

Simplify with Low-Maintenance Plants

It is all about ease as we age. We've lived too long to continue doing things the hard way. Since none of us want to give up gardening, we need to look for ways to simplify our lives as well as our gardens.

This is the promise I made to myself:

I will stop finding room for every plant I fall in love with. I will look for plants that make my heart sing, are low maintenance, and give me the biggest bang for my buck.

A good rule of thumb is to strive for 60–70 percent low-maintenance plants. Group your few high-maintenance plants at strategic places like the front porch so they give a good punch of color but are easy to

Simplify your garden with fewer plants and more mulch.

reach. Plant species that are adaptable to your microclimate, be it cold, frost, or heat (I must continually remind myself not to buy any new plants unless they can withstand an occasional frost). Last, but not least, when you remove a plant because it's unhappy, don't feel like you have to replace it right away (or ever). You could spread some mulch and call it a day.

Here are some aspects to keep in mind about different plants you might be considering for your garden:

☐ *Annuals. While they don't require a lot of maintenance once they're planted, annuals do need to be replaced at the end of the season (unless you have a mild winter and they re-seed in the spring), which means more work. This took me a while to accept, because each season I'd be seduced by the riot of colorful blooms, but planting a lot of annuals is not low-maintenance or friendly to my budget every year.*

☐ *Perennials are beautiful and can last for years, but they require deadheading to stimulate re-blooming, and eventually you'll probably need to add plant supports. Every couple of years, you'll also need to divide them and transplant them to other parts of your garden (or you can give them away, which can be fun).*

☐ *Flowering shrubs are easy to maintain with one annual pruning. Prune summer- and fall-flowering shrubs in the dormant season and prune spring-flowering trees and shrubs after they're done flowering.*

☐ *Trees don't require a great deal of maintenance aside from deep watering young trees. If you plant new fruit trees, choose ultra-dwarf varieties or those that will do well in containers.*

☐ *Grasses. Plant fewer flowering species and more grasses. Once established, grasses are drought tolerant. And they're available in a wide range of colors and textures, which give year-round beauty.*

☐ *Succulents. It's no wonder succulent sales have soared in the past decade. Succulents are perfect for drought conditions and are as low maintenance as you can get. They need infrequent water and an annual or semi-annual pruning around the edges. Then they give you pups that you can re-plant or gift to friends.*

☐ *Herbs. If you grow nothing else, grow herbs. They can really enhance your quality of life by giving every meal a fresh flavor. And they're not only useful in the kitchen but beautiful in a garden, providing a lovely fragrance, and usually requiring little water. Many tolerate poor soil and hillsides, and some perennial herbs last for years. Plant them and trim as you use them, and they'll just keep on doing what they were meant to do.*

☐ *Edible flowers are the easiest flowers to grow. Put in nasturtium once, and you'll have orange and gold flowers with gorgeous green leaves for years to come.*

☐ *Bulbs are under-utilized in many gardens. Spring bulbs multiply year after year, and are as "no maintenance" as plants get. They're fun to use in pots for bursts of color during the rainy season.*

☐ *Groundcovers. As long as these low-growing spreaders get occasional water and you've planted them close together enough, they'll block out weeds, doing that maintenance job for you.*

QUICK AND EASY SEASONAL PLANTING

There's nothing I relish more than saving time and energy. My friend Heidi feels exactly the same way. She loves to have blooming flowers year round (we're lucky that our mild climate allows this) in certain places and especially in front of the fountain she sculpted years ago. She came up with an idea I think is brilliant that allows her to swap out color from one season to the next.

She dug a trough deep enough to hold several one-gallon pots and inserted them empty. Then she surrounded the pots with bark and ran a drip irrigation line across them all. When she is ready for a change she removes the old plants from the pots in the ground, inserts new gallon-sized plants, and voila! She has a new look without any digging.

This method works in window boxes too. It saves you digging up old roots and schlepping bags of soil to replace them—instead, the planting is permanently set up. Heidi prefers using annuals because they have the longest blooming season, but this could work just as easily with perennials.

LEFT: *The pots, with drip irrigation set up, stay in place as you swap the plants out.*

RIGHT: *Easy color, and the foliage hides your methods.*

*A place for everything and
everything in its place.*

BEN FRANKLIN

Clear the Clutter

By keeping a tidy garden, where everything has its place, you'll save time and energy because you'll always know where to find everything you need. You'll save money because you won't have to replace tools you think have been lost. Above all, by eliminating clutter, you reduce potential safety issues. The same principles apply to your storage spaces.

Clean out your garage and tool shed to eliminate anything you could trip on. Keep only the things you need that speak to your heart. Take the plunge and get rid of the rest.

Add pegboards and shelves at a height that's easy to reach—measure from the floor to the top of your head to judge the maximum height you should store anything.

Get in the habit of putting away your tools after each use and never leave them out because you never know when it might rain. Rusted tools will be costly to replace.

If you start to feel overwhelmed by de-cluttering, attack the job one shelf or drawer at a time.

As you clear the clutter, categorize items into five groups:

1 Keep it

2 Give it away

3 Sell it

4 Donate it

5 Let it go (into the trash—sometimes items have reached the end of their usefulness)

NOTE: There is no "maybe" pile.

TONI'S TIP

═══════════

Avoid Adirondack chairs because they force your hips to be lower than your knees, making it too hard to get up and out.

Seating in the Shade

Have you noticed one of the not so great joys of aging is how susceptible we become to temperatures? It's because our bodies become less efficient at regulating body heat. When external temperatures rise, like when we're exposed to direct sunlight or extremely hot environments, so does our internal body temperature. This is why seniors suffer from heat stroke more often than younger gardeners.

Combat this reality by creating seating in the shade for taking breaks in hot weather. Here are some things to consider:

☐ *Make sure your chairs or benches are comfortable and have backs.*

☐ *Many trees are messy because they drop their leaves all year, but they can be worth keeping because they also provide shade during the hottest months.*

BELOW: *Shade sails are perfect for seasonal shade.*

OPPOSITE: *A delightful place to take a break.*

☐ *Add a pergola or gazebo with seating for mess-free, year-round shade and to add visual interest.*

☐ *Incorporate umbrellas throughout your garden. They're easy to pop up or take down as needed.*

☐ *Decorative shade sails are a cost-effective alternative to awnings and can easily be removed when winter sets in. Due to their popularity, you can probably find a decent one at most home goods stores.*

☐ *Check out Pinterest for other fun shade ideas.*

Rise up! Raise Those Beds!

If you have a bad back or similar limited mobility issues, it might be time to bring your garden UP, eliminating the need to stoop or bend over. If your knees keep you from kneeling, raise up your beds and plant from sitting or standing.

Good reasons to use raised beds:

☐ *Fewer pest problems*

☐ *Minimal weeds*

☐ *Improved drainage*

☐ *Increased visibility for gardeners with compromised vision*

☐ *Easier to reach across to plant, maintain, and harvest*

When you incorporate raised beds, think about your comfort level:

☐ *Can you walk and/or stand for short periods of time?*

☐ *Do you use a walking aid such as a cane or walker?*

☐ *Can you sit for long periods of time?*

☐ *Are you in a wheelchair?*

☐ *Would you benefit from a grab bar?*

☐ *Do you need handrails?*

OPPOSITE:
A waist-high bed makes maintenance and harvesting a cinch.

LEFT: *These raised beds have been built to last a long time.*

RIGHT: *This raised bed is the perfect height for gardeners in wheelchairs.*

☐ *How far can you comfortably reach?*

☐ *Are your upper extremities, lower extremities, or both affected?*

☐ *Do you have visual or other sensory issues?*

Consider the following guidelines for a good raised bed, and then design your raised bed so it will be comfortable, functional, and accessible for you and your needs.

☐ *Raised beds should be no deeper than 10–12 inches deep and not more than 3–4 feet wide.*

☐ *If your raised beds are built of lumber, consider adding a foot-wide smooth edge to create a seating area to relieve tired legs and a place to lay tools.*

☐ *Elevated raised beds are easiest on backs when then are as close as possible to waist high. Many raised beds on the market are only*

20–28 inches high, which may not be high enough if you are in a wheelchair, you incorporate a chair, or it has a ledge to sit on.

☐ If you use a wheelchair, make sure you provide knee space beneath the beds.

☐ Add soaker hoses or drip irrigation lines and install timers.

Elevate with Containers

One of the best ways of dealing with pain is to bring your plants up closer to you by incorporating containers in your garden. Think how much easier your edibles and ornamentals will be to monitor, maintain, and harvest when they're elevated.

Creating an easy care accessible container garden starts with an adaptive design. Where are containers needed for impact and architectural interest? How tall should they be so you can comfortably sit next to them?

Container gardening doesn't require a lot of effort or space once you decide on the best placement and you choose the right pots. This is especially great for gardeners living in condos or apartments with balconies, or for small decks, patios, and yards. Like raised beds, containers are easier to weed and water than gardens in the ground.

I love growing food, especially tomatoes and salad greens, in containers because I have fewer problems with insects and pests, and I don't have to worry about poor soil conditions. In addition, a salad

Keep in Mind

You can find more information on wheelchair-accessible gardens by googling *enabled gardens* or *accessible gardens* for the disabled. The term *handicapped* is more prevalent in the United States, whereas *disabled* is used in the United Kingdom and Europe.

SQUARE FOOT GARDENS

Our first attempt at growing veggies was a square foot garden in our front yard based on the ground-breaking (pardon the pun) book *Square Foot Gardening*, by Mel Bartholomew. Mel's book is perfect for veggie novices. He breaks each task down and helps you understand each plant's requirements and how to do succession planting. The part we liked best? There is little or no weeding!

Since my wonderful bad back (thanks, Mom) doesn't allow for heavy digging and our yard is

Square foot gardening comes with its own success formula. Here are a couple, planted as Mel would have done it.

pretty small, square foot gardening seemed like the perfect solution for us. We followed Mel's advice precisely as we installed a 4×4 square foot garden on the ground. We had a lot of fun choosing which veggies to plant and how to plant them. His soil mixture was easy to incorporate, and he was right, we had few weeds and no pests. Our small square foot garden worked great for two years, and we were pleased with our harvest.

Year three, everything changed. My husband desperately needed knee replacement surgery and my back was out, again, which meant neither of us could get down on the ground to maintain our plants.

Needless to say, our second square foot garden was an elevated raised bed on legs, which made planting and maintenance a whole lot easier for our knees and backs. Depending on your height and the height of your raised bed, you can stand or sit while you garden—it's perfect for someone in a wheelchair.

garden container can be moved around in order to catch more sun or shade as needed or to avoid extreme weather conditions. It's fun to mix seasonal flowers in your salad containers, so you have a beautiful pop of color between your leafy greens.

Here are some tips to think about:

☐ *Containers are great for marking the end of an area for safety, such as at the end of a path or at the bottom of stairs.*

☐ *Use pots to hide ugly electrical outlets, an air conditioner unit, or anything else you'd rather not see.*

☐ *Incorporate risers of varying heights to make your container display more interesting and to improve drainage.*

☐ *Avoid using saucers so your containers' feet don't stay wet. They hate that!*

FROM LEFT: *Ceramic pots come in vibrant colors and are built to last.*

Galvanized metal planters give a clean, modern look.

Coordinating terra cotta pots.

- Put your largest plant in the largest pot and echo the pot's lines with similar shapes and colors.

- Light-colored pots can lighten up a dark garden or corner.

- Add a trellis for growing beans, peas, climbing roses, or clematis.

- It's less work to fill a container with soil than to compost an in-ground garden.

- Another benefit of container salad gardening is being able to plant once but harvest multiple times. Leafy greens can be cut down almost to ground level and will re-grow additional leaves for a continuous harvest, allowing you to enjoy three or four harvests from each plant, saving you time, money, and energy.

TONI'S TIP

Keep a lightweight chair, stool, or reversible kneeler seat next to your containers so you can maintain them while seated, eliminating back or knee pain.

Choose the Right Container

Choose your containers wisely—the right one can make all the difference. Size and weight should be your first determining factor, especially if you are gardening on a balcony. You have a lot of container options to choose from and each has its advantages.

First, consider your climate. If your area gets frost, a ceramic or concrete pot may crack in the winter, so look for synthetic fiberglass or plastic pots, which are lighter and easier to move. You can always put the synthetic pot inside a decorative pot, which will provide better protection from the elements as long as both pots have drainage holes.

If you live in a drought climate, high-fired ceramic pots and plastic pots do not insulate the soil and roots from the heat. Adding mulch on top keeps the moisture in.

	Durable	Lightweight	Colorful
Concrete/Cast Stone	x		
Galvanized	x		
Glazed Ceramic	x		x
Half Wine Barrels			
Terra Cotta	x	x	
Wood		x	
Fiberglass/Resin	x	x	x
Plastic	x	x	x
Fabric Grow Pots		x	

The table below will help you decide the best container for your needs.
Listed from heaviest to lightest

CONCRETE, also known as cast stone, is the heaviest option and lasts a long time. Concrete pots are often left natural or finished with a water-based stain in neutral tones.

GALVANIZED METAL PLANTERS. Initially used as horse feeding troughs, these have become popular for vegetables gardens, and they give a clean, modern look.

CERAMIC. There are so many gorgeous colors, sizes, and designs to choose from amongst glazed and unglazed ceramic pots. They will last for many years to come.

Long-lasting	Shows Wear	Economical	Porosity	Low or No Maintenance
x	x	x	x	x
x				x
x				x
		x		
x		x	x	x
	x		x	x
x				x
x		x		x
	x	x	x	x

HALF WINE BARRELS. These are classic planters for all kinds of edibles and ornamentals. After you drill holes for drainage, spray the interior with apple cider vinegar to inhibit the growth of fungus.

TERRA COTTA or clay. If you love the look, as I do, there's no option more beautiful than Italian terra cotta. They can last for decades (and do in many Italian villages). Clay pots dry out faster than other options, so you may need to water deeply several times a week. Regardless, these are my favorites.

WOOD PLANTERS come in a wide range. Those made of cedar or redwood have become expensive, but they will last. Lesser quality wood planters need a plastic liner to prevent leaks or they will split when wet.

FIBERGLASS OR RESIN POTS. These days can choose from a large assortment of lightweight containers that really do look like stone and terra cotta. You might have to knock on them to determine if they're the real deal or not.

PLASTIC. Some gardeners love to garden with plastic pots, because they prevent water loss through evaporation, and there is a large assortment to choose from.

FABRIC GROW POTS. A number of different fabric pot brands have proliferated on the market of late (cannabis growers love them). They're great if weight is an issue. Be aware the salts from water can leach through the fabric, making these pots unsightly with time.

ABOVE: *The bigger the pot the more color you can put into it.*

OPPOSITE: *These pots are ready to move on demand.*

Size (and Shape) Matters

Size does matter with containers. BUY POTS AS BIG AS YOU CAN AFFORD. Why? The larger the container, the more volume roots have to spread, especially for annuals, like indeterminate tomatoes, some of which require pots as large as 24 inches wide. In addition, big pots are the focal point in your garden, and the best way to start a container garden.

Make sure your pots are a minimum of 12 inches deep and look for one that's taller than it is wide. Those lovely, low bowls are great for shallow-rooted flowers or salad greens and lettuces, and, of course, succulents, but they aren't deep enough for most plants. Additionally, shallow pots and low bowls dry out quicker and may need daily watering.

Choose a pot that's wider at the top than at the bottom. Many gardeners find out why this is important the hard way. If you find you need to remove a plant from a pot that is narrow at the top, the sad truth is you may need to break the pot to get the plant out.

Drain, Baby, Drain

If you only remember one thing about using containers, let it be this: they must have drainage.

Don't use saucers with your containers. Most plants prefer well-drained soils and will die from root rot if the soil is consistently wet. Also, the standing water in saucers can attract mosquitos, which makes your garden less pleasant. Instead, use pot feet, risers, casters, or trivets to elevate each pot so it can drain efficiently.

Moving Those Puppies

As the sun changes through summer and winter months, you might want to move your containers to better locations. You also might choose to bring them inside when the weather turns inclement. Pot casters are an ideal way to move your containers where you want them (they're also a great way to elevate your containers for drainage). Be sure to buy casters that have a locking mechanism so you don't find yourself chasing your pots down the driveway!

When planting a container you intend to move, place packing peanuts, empty plastic bottles, or even wood chips (to retain moisture) into the bottom third of the pot to take up space and reduce the weight. Cover them with nylon netting before adding the remaining potting soil. Most plants need only 10–12 inches of soil.

Re-Cycle, Re-Use, Re-Purpose

It's time to rethink your pre-loved things. Any vessel that can hold soil and has drainage will work as a planter. Look in your attic or your garage to find those dusty mementos, which you can't bear to part with. Go to garage sales to find unique, interesting objects.

You can make a planter out of just about anything. An old washing machine drum painted a bold color is a fun container—so are old wagons and wheelbarrows, sinks, trophies, old boots, even file cabinets. I cracked up when I saw an old toilet that had been beautifully painted and tiled, with the bowl made into a fountain and the tank a planter.

Anything can be used as a planter, as long as it has drainage.

SELF-WATERING PLANTERS

No matter what material they're made of, self-watering planters can immediately make your life as a gardener easier. They take the guesswork out of watering for weeks at a time and save you from doing the task manually. A skeptical gardener friend of mine has been testing her self-watering planters for three months and is now ready to leave for a month long trip to Provence without worrying if her plants will survive or not.

Self-watering containers have an inner pot that holds the plant and the soil and an outer pot or bottom reservoir that holds the water. When the soil gets dry, a wick delivers moisture to the roots of the plant as needed.

The only disadvantage to self-watering planters is the possibility of mosquitoes breeding in the water reservoir, but this can be avoided by adding a couple drops of oil to the water every time you refill.

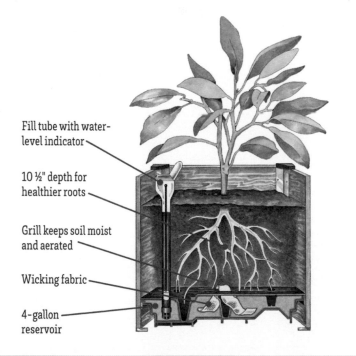

Fill tube with water-level indicator

10 ½" depth for healthier roots

Grill keeps soil moist and aerated

Wicking fabric

4-gallon reservoir

A quick internet search will turn up many recycled planter ideas. All you have to do is make sure they are wide enough and deep enough to grow plants in, and make sure you can drill a hole to create drainage. With recycled and re-purposed planters, you are only limited by your imagination—and drainage (always drainage).

Vertical Gardening

No space? No problem. Grow your flowers and veggies up, by finding inventive vertical gardening opportunities.

It's refreshing to know you can garden without having to bend down. Vertical gardening is a technique of growing plants in hanging baskets, tomato cages, fences, walls, bamboo stakes, arbors, pergolas, and trellises so most of the maintenance is at waist-to-eye-level, enabling you to stand or sit to maintain and harvest your edibles and ornamentals. This is easy eye-level gardening at its best.

Not only is it physically easier to garden this way it also saves you space, allowing for more flowers and vegetables on a balcony or deck.

You have a large variety of vertical planters to choose from, depending where you want to use them. Here are a few to choose from:

☐ *Window Boxes are a great way to raise up your plantings. I prefer the heavy duty metal ones with coir liners. Coir is a material made from the inner husk of coconuts. Be sure the coir liner you buy comes to the top of your container when it's filled with soil and plants. If it doesn't, expect leaks every time you water.*

Nothing is impossible.
The word itself says I'm possible.

AUDREY HEPBURN

FOR SUCCESS WITH VERTICAL PLANTERS, FOLLOW THESE SIMPLE DIRECTIONS:

1 Fill each cavity halfway with the appropriate potting mix (or cactus mix, if you are planting succulents).

2 Add your plants and more soil, tamping the soil down as you plant.

3 Two or three times a week, tamp the soil down and water them thoroughly. This is where patience comes in handy—before you can hang the planters, they really do need to stay horizontal for a few weeks while the roots take hold.

4 When they seem settled in, ask a friend to help hanging them up. Then stand back and admire your new vertical garden.

CARING FOR YOUR VERTICAL GARDENS:

☐ Use an extended-handle hose sprayer for watering or add a drip irrigation line and timer.

☐ Find a way to contain the water runoff from your plants so you don't make a mess or drip on the balcony downstairs.

TOP LEFT: *Harvesting squash has never been easier than from an arbor.*

BOTTOM LEFT: *A coir liner in an iron basket makes for a beautiful display.*

RIGHT: *A salad wall looks great and makes dinner a breeze.*

142

☐ *Trellises abound, in a huge array of sizes, styles, colors, and designs. Install your trellises away from whatever wall or fence you're covering—this allows your plants to grow with proper air circulation. In my garden, I added a small wooden block to the wall and screwed my trellis to that. Tomato cages, bamboo stakes, fences, walls, and arbors all serve a similar function to trellises, helping vining plants grow upward.*

☐ *Railing planters are the best thing to happen to condo and apartment dwellers who can't use a nail to hang planters. There are some fabulous and colorful self-watering planters that simply sit over a railing, giving you an instant garden.*

☐ *Pergolas and arbors are perfect for growing climbing roses, wisteria, grapes, and even squash and vining fruits and vegetables, because they are constructed to be strong and sturdy.*

☐ *Living wall vertical planters have been popular for the last several years, mainly because they're super effective for growing shallow-rooted plants and because they save space while you grow salad greens, lettuces and, most particularly, succulents*

YOUR TOOLS

The most noteworthy thing about gardeners is that they are always optimistic, always enterprising, and never satisfied. They always look forward to doing something better than they have ever done before.

VITA SACKVILLE-WEST

Give Yourself a Hand

Gardeners love their tools and every gardener has a favorite tool they cannot garden without. However, many senior gardeners report the older they get, the weaker and less flexible their hands become, which is a problem because you need your hands to do literally every task in your garden. *Your hands are your most important tools.* So what happens when your favorite tool is no longer comfortable due to physical issues with your most important tools?

The first step is to accept what's going on with your body and acknowledge your strengths and weaknesses. The five most common causes for pain, inflammation, and weakness in the hands are arthritis, muscle loss, carpal tunnel, tendinitis, and post-stroke powerlessness.

This section will, first, give you ideas about how to adapt your tools at home for pennies on the dollar and, second, suggest new ergonomic tools that can be the difference between pain and joy when you work in your garden.

We All Need Ergonomics

Garden tool manufacturers are responding to the vast number of senior gardeners who need garden tools that are easier on their hands, backs, knees, and wrists. New ergonomic tools, designed to create less stress on muscles and joints, are appearing on the market all the time. These tools are safer and easier to use than conventional options, and comfort is their highest priority. Ergonomic tools have large, soft handles, which helps you get a better grip and encourages proper form. They're crafted to fit in your hand better and are made from lightweight, durable materials. You might love your tried and true wood-handle steel spade, but once you use one made from cast aluminum with a fiberglass shaft and finished with a comfortable, non-slip grip, you'll understand why I'm suggesting a change.

Ergonomically designed hand trowels, weeders, and cultivators are designed with handles that keep your wrist in a straight line rather than bent in a way that can cause pain. Other ergonomic options help you to keep your back straight—not bending over and not twisted. These tools are lightweight and balanced in your hand. There's one in a size that is perfect for you.

DIY Your Favorite Tools

Now is the time to take a good long look at your tools and perhaps change the way you think about them. Do they help you do what needs to be done? Your number one goal should always be comfort. If you've kept certain tools because they have sentimental value, but you know in your heart, they aren't as comfortable to use as they used to be, it may be time to re-think what they're doing for you. If you find you cannot part with them, perhaps you can find a creative way to display them so you can see them often.

A good tool will conform to your hand, rather than your hand, or wrist, conforming to the tool. If a tool is rusty, it won't work well for you (and the rust will return unless you are constantly diligent). Rusty tools should be the first ones you replace.

But wait! If you have a favorite tool you love but haven't been able to use because of a limited mobility issue, change it. Make it work for you. You can adapt the tools you own, often for free or for very little money, which is great if you are on a budget and still want tools you can use for years to come.

BUYER ALERT

Some manufacturers may claim to be ergonomically designed, but it doesn't go much farther than marketing language. Let your comfort indicate how ergonomically designed a tool is for you.

LEFT: *My retired
watering can
collection.*

OPPOSITE: *My old
trowel got new life
with cushioning
from an old
bicycle grip.*

Beyond the tips and techniques for adapted tools here, be creative! Think outside the tool and adapt these or other ideas elsewhere in your arsenal.

DIY: CUSHY LOVE HANDLES

A large, soft grip is the single most important element of a tool for those of us with pain or decreased muscle strength in our hands.

When I found myself dealing with these symptoms, I took my old trowel down to a local bike store and asked them if they had any bike grips they were going to throw away. They gave me one and I was able to force it on to the handle of my old favorite trowel. Presto! It was immediately more comfortable to use, because it was cushy and the grip was enlarged. It cost me nothing.

You can cushion the handles on any of your tools, even bucket handles, with duct tape or cushioned tape, like the kind used to wrap tennis racket or baseball bat handles. Some gardeners like to use foam or pieces of pipe insulation. Even those large foam hair curlers from back in the day, can enlarge the size and the softness of a handle, if glued on securely. Any added cushioning makes gripping much easier.

DIY: ADD COLOR TO HANDLES
Have you ever lost a tool because you didn't see it in the debris and then accidentally threw it away? Has anyone accidentally (or not) taken one of your tools? The solution is to change the color of your tools' grips to make them easier to find.

LEFT: *This metal tool gets too hot to touch when it's in the sun.*

RIGHT: *Once the rubber coating dries, this handle will be comfortable to hold at any temperature.*

At a seminar I gave in Mill Valley, a woman who had recently remodeled her garden introduced me to a product called Plasti-Dip. She said she liked to work alongside the workers she hired so she could stay engaged in case they had questions. Things went well—they were good guys who seemed to know what they were doing. But at some point, she noticed two of her tools had disappeared.

Plasti-Dip to the rescue! An air-dry, liquid plasticized rubber coating for the handles of your tools, it's super easy to use and the end result is a softer, rubberized, and, most importantly, colorful, easy-grip cushion that prevents slipping. This clever lady dipped all her remaining tool handles in pink, and guess what? She never lost another tool.

TONI'S TIP

If you can, plan to dip all your handles at one time. The container isn't air tight so leftover product may dry up. You can try pouring the remaining liquid into different, air tight container, but why risk it or do the prep work more than once?

You can buy this handy product at your local hardware store. It comes in more than fifty colors, so let your imagination flow. I bet purple would be nice. If the hardware store doesn't have the color you want, ask them if they will special order it for you.

DIY: HELP WITH VISION ISSUES

One of the most important measurements in gardening relates to planting bulbs of all sizes. You need to know how deep you're planting them, which can be difficult to judge if your vision isn't what it used to be. A simple solution? Drill holes on your trowel at 1-inch intervals. This lets you feel the depth as you push the tool down into the earth.

Holes drilled into a trowel blade let you feel how deep you're planting bulbs.

Another tip for vision issues: as you replace your hoses, buy colorful ones you can see easily, so you don't accidentally trip over them.

DIY: NO-BEND PLANTING

Gardeners with bad backs will do almost anything to avoid having to bend over. Am I right? One of the many times my back went out was, of course, the week I wanted to plant bulbs. Since I couldn't bend down to do the job I needed a workaround. I found the solution in a leftover piece of PVC pipe from my tool shed. Here's how to achieve no-bend planting for yourself:

1 Find a piece of PVC wide enough for your bulbs to fit through.

2 Cut it waist high, then cut both ends on a diagonal. If you are in a wheelchair or prefer to do this kind of a project seated, have the pipe cut to the height of your seated waist.

3 Mark inches using a permanent marker.

4 In the garden, use the pipe (or your favorite tool) to dig holes to the proper depth for your bulbs.

CLOCKWISE FROM TOP: *First, use the PVC to create a furrow for planting seeds.*

Then drop a seed down the pipe.

By moving the PVC along, you can easily plant all your seeds without bending over.

5. Drop one bulb through the center of your pipe (pointy end of the bulb sticking up, but you knew that).

6. Move the appropriate distance and repeat to plant the rest of your bulbs.

7. When you're finished, you can use the PVC to cover the bulbs with soil.

8. PVC is good for planting seeds too! Just drag the pipe along the soil to make a furrow. Then go back and drop your seeds through the pipe at appropriate intervals. When you're finished seeding, use the PVC to cover up your new babies with soil.

TONI'S TIP

Planting tiny seeds? Pour them into a spice jar with holes in the lid and sprinkle them in your garden or raised bed. Then you can use the PVC pipe or a rake to cover the seeds with soil.

Get a Grip!

Remember, comfort is key when it comes to grip. Good ergonomics will prevent injury and give you the best results even with diminished hand strength. If padded handles on your favorite tools don't solve every grip-related challenge you face, here are some more ideas on how to give your hands a hand.

ADD-ON ASSISTIVE DEVICES

D-GRIP is an add-on interchangeable adaptive aid for long-handled tools like hoes, push brooms, and shovels. It attaches mid-way down the shaft of the tool—place it where your hand comfortably falls.

When you shovel, for example, incorporating a D-grip keeps your wrists in a neutral position and it gives lifting leverage to your forward hand, which makes lifting easier. It also helps with lower back issues because it reduces bending over while using the tool.

LEFT: *Attach your D-grip mid-shaft where it feels comfortable for you.*

RIGHT: *A T-grip near the top of a broom makes sweeping easier.*

T-GRIP is the D-grip's little sister. A T-grip attaches towards the top of the handle and is designed to give pushing and pulling control to your back hand when you are sweeping, raking, or vacuuming. It keeps your wrist in a neutral position, and will reduce blisters. Because you are using both hands, it also takes the pressure off your back.

BRAND LOYALTY: EASI-GRIP TOOLS

Easi-Grip tools have been made in Britain since 1975 by an organization called PETA UK. PETA stands for: Practical Ergonomic and Therapeutic Aids and their tools and aids are Occupational Therapy approved.

The Easi-Grip tools all have a natural grip and exclusive ninety-degree perpendicular handle, which keeps your wrist neutral and in perfect alignment. You can buy them individually or as a set with a

fork, cultivator, trowel, and weeder. They are also available in a long reach version.

The Easi-Grip Arm Cuff is a forearm brace that makes your arm do the work with less stress on your wrists because it acts as a counter balance for increased comfort and leverage for digging. These are especially useful if you suffer from arthritis or carpal tunnel.

If your back, wrists, and hands need extra support, you might want to consider buying the removable and adjustable Easi-Grip Add-on Handle. It attaches to any tool (up to 1.5" diameter) with two adjustable stainless steel clamps. And if you think outside the garden, they can help you reduce strain on your joints when used indoors with vacuums and dust mops.

All Easi-Grip tools come with a lifetime manufacturer's warranty.

TOP LEFT: *The perpendicular handle of this trowel helps protect your wrist.*

BOTTOM LEFT: *An Easi-Grip fork and arm cuff in action.*

RIGHT: *Long-reach grip tools make ground-level tasks easy. The arm cuff adds increased comfort.*

ABOVE: *Weeds don't stand a chance against the Radius weeder.*

OPPOSITE: *Save your shoulders with long reach tools.*

BRAND LOYALTY: RADIUS GRIP

The first time I saw a Radius Tool was at a garden trade show and I have to say, I thought they were funny looking. But I overheard two nursery buyers talking about the line, and they were raving about the tools they've sold in their stores. I bought one and realized why they look the way they do. Radius is all about ergonomics and comfort.

These tools maximize comfort while minimizing hand and wrist stress. Their exclusive design helps transfer energy from large muscles directly to the blades of the tool while allowing you to maintain a neutral wrist. Another real plus is the light weight and exceptional strength of their aluminum blades.

They offer a trowel, transplanter, weeder, scooper, and cultivator. I personally love the weeder because the serrated blade cuts through even the toughest clay soil and the curved fulcrum is great for popping out even the most stubborn weeds.

Best of all, they come with a lifetime guarantee. Oh, oh, oh … one more thing! Radius tools come in yummy colors, like purple, so you won't lose them in your garden.

No Pain, All Gain: Long-Reach Tools

There is no longer a need to risk straining your neck, back, shoulders, or arms when pruning, raking or working your garden. Long reach tools are a fabulous resource for gardeners who need to reach across their garden beds and raised beds with ease. Whether you need a trowel, cultivator, fork or hoe, get a gauge of what length you need and look around before you buy. You will find a number of brands available with long shafts ranging from 24 to 35 inches.

Long-handled tools as well as extended handles on tools decrease the need to reach beyond what is comfortable and keeps gardeners from bending over, and they encourage using two hands, which will improve leverage.

BRAND LOYALTY:
COBRAHEAD WEEDER AND CULTIVATOR

The CobraHead Long Handle Weeder and Cultivator offers enough reach to let you weed while standing up. Yay! I love it because it works in tight spaces and breaks down soil more easily than a wide hoe or multi-tined tool. Its comfortably designed handle can be used if you are left-handed or right-handed, and it has an exception-ally strong steel blade that can plow right through the heaviest of clay soils. The blade looks like the head of a cobra snake and acts like a fingernail to pry things up. I am amazed at how it makes weeding less of a drag!

BRAND LOYALTY: FISKARS NO-BEND WEEDER

I've been searching for the perfect no-bend weeder for years. A while back, I ordered one online. After an hour of squinting to read the eight point font instructions and trying to assemble the darned thing, I gave up. As good fortune would have it, that night, two of our friends came over for dinner. They saw what I was trying to do and offered to help. An hour and a half later, it was assembled, but it still didn't work. I sent it back and got a refund. The best way to know if a tool is going to work for you, is to try them out in person before buying.

The gardening gods were looking down on me when I found the One. It's made by Fiskars and it comes assembled (what a concept!). It even has the instructions printed on the side of the tool in large print. This no-bend weeder removes weeds and the entire root, without bending down, making a weed-free garden or lawn easier than ever.

Lightweight and simple to use, it comes with a lifetime warranty and boasts an *Ease of Use* stamp of approval by the Arthritis

BELOW LEFT:
Finally, a no-bend weeder that's easy to use and no assembly required.

BELOW RIGHT:
Holds weeds securely to make them easy to toss.

159

YOUR TOOLS

HOW THIS NO-BEND WEEDER WORKS

Just place the head over a weed, step down on the reinforced foot platform, and the four serrated, stainless-steel claws grab the weed by the root for clean removal. An offset handle reduces wrist strain, a viewing window in the pedal makes claw placement mistake-free, and an easy-eject mechanism clears the head between uses for quick, easy, and fun cleanup.

OPPOSITE LEFT:
One rake to rule them all.

OPPOSITE RIGHT:
A great tool if you are vertically challenged or don't want to bend down.

Foundation. The handle was designed to reduce wrist strain and help with a better grip. A fun bonus feature is the eject mechanism that shoots your freshly pulled weed into the debris can, making a game of basketball out of a very boring task.

Expandable Rake

I love my expandable rake. I finally gave away my heavy, bulky, old fashioned rakes and just use this one for all my raking chores. It's made of aluminum, so it's lightweight, and it has a telescoping, extendable handle, which makes hanging it up off the ground for easy storage and eliminates a potential tripping hazard.

What I like best, though, are its expandable tines. They can go from 7 to 21 inches wide. Let's say you want to pick up leaves without disturbing the mulch beneath. By adjusting the tines fairly wide, you can rake the leaves and leave the mulch in place. Then, if you're in a confined area, like in between containers, you can close the tines to 7 inches and rake in between without getting up again. Easy squeezy . . . uh, expandy!

Reaching Aids

Sometimes called Grabbers, reaching aids can be a great help when you need to pick up something from the ground without bending over. If you are vertically challenged, like some people I know, it can also help getting a box of fertilizer from the top shelf of your tool shed

without using a ladder or stepstool. If you have a choice, buy one with suction cups—they're easier to use.

If the Glove Fits, Wear It!

When you wear gloves, your hands and cuticles won't get dried out and cracked the way gloveless hands do. Gloves also protect your hands from bruises and scratches. For anybody with diabetes or allergies, or anybody who takes blood thinners or has circulatory problems, wearing gloves is an easy, no-brainer way to avoid infection when working in the garden. Also, it's okay to admit, wearing gloves has cosmetic benefits too. I wear gloves to prevent those yucky purple senile purpura and cuts from thorns but also to protect my manicure.

Here are a couple things to consider when buying gloves:

PROPER FIT: Gloves need to fit snug but not too tight. Your fingers should be near the end of the fingertip but not about to bust through. If you can't bend your fingers, make a fist, or completely stretch open your hand comfortably, that pair is not for you.

GOOD CONSTRUCTION: Gloves should have smooth, well-constructed seams so they're comfortable to wear for long periods of time. Double stitched seams are best, but if the seams feel bulky, don't buy them—they won't be comfortable over the long haul.

BUYING ONLINE: If you want to buy your gloves online, do it only if they have a sizing guide you can print out and lay your hand on to determine the best fit for you. It's really best to buy at a store so you can try them on.

OPPOSITE: *Keep your hands protected but your fingers nimble.*

START A COLLECTION: If you find a pair you really like, buy a second pair, in case one gets damaged. I am a firm believer there is a glove for every job in the garden, but in case you don't have money to buy every glove on your wish list, I'll discuss the three essential styles below.

BRAND LOYALTY: SMART GRIP GLOVES

The first glove I recommend is one you can wear for day-in-day-out work in the garden. It should be lightweight and made of nylon or nitrile, making them washable and durable. If it has a sticky surface to help with gripping, all the better. Nitrile is a good way to go if you need waterproof gloves, but if it's hot out, they can make your hands sweat.

I love my lightweight Smart Grip gloves from Garden Works USA, because they fit like a second skin, which helps me feel the difference between a live leaf and a dead leaf when I'm dead-heading or weeding. They have textured grips to prevent blisters

TONI'S TIP

When it comes to wearing gloves . . . JUST DO IT.

and minimize dropping tools. Carbon fiber fingertips mean you can use them to answer your smart phone or use a touch screen without removing your gloves. They are made of nylon, which is breathable, even in hot weather, and they're washable. Other reliable brands: Duluth, Mud Gloves, Atlas, and Foxgloves.

BRAND LOYALTY: TRADITIONS WORK GLOVES

The second glove every gardener should own is a pair for heavy-duty gardening—something strong enough for when you're using large tools, especially power tools. Here are some things to look for:

REINFORCED FINGERTIPS. What's the first part of any glove to wear out or accidentally get cut off? It's always the fingers. Think of that extra layer of reinforcement as extra protection for your fingers.

PADDING. For the best protection, a good work glove should have padding on the palm, fingertips, and knuckles.

VELCRO WRIST CLOSURE. Keep soil and debris out of your gloves. Make sure the closure is adjustable and comfortable at your wrist or above.

MATERIALS. You can find good work gloves made from a variety of materials—the best ones are goatskin, pigskin, cowhide leather, or synthetic leather. Avoid cotton gloves because they offer no protection for your hands and their seams give out quickly.

I like Traditions gloves by Garden Works USA because they're exceptionally well made, with a goatskin palm and the added protection of Velcro wrist closure to keep the soil out and the gloves on. They also have reinforced fingertips to protect your fingers from sharp objects, thorns, and any nails you may encounter. Other brands to try: Woman's Work, Magid, and Gold Leaf waterproof gloves.

BRAND LOYALTY: LEATHER PRO'S GAUNTLET GLOVES
A good gauntlet glove covers your forearm, has padded palms and finger pads that improve your gripping power and reduce calluses and blisters, and gives you the ultimate protection when pruning roses, thorny lemon trees, overgrown berries, sharp tips of succulents, or even clearing brush.

Many gauntlets are made of calfskin, pigskin or goatskin, like the Leather Pro's by Garden Works USA I have used for years. They also sell Comfort Pros, which are made from synthetic leather and are allergy free and washable.

A good rose gauntlet sleeve will provide superior thorn protection and should come up to your elbow or close to it. Gauntlets cost more than others but they are worth the investment. Mine saved me

from cutting off my finger! After that could-have-been-horrible experience, I never go near my thorny roses, lemon tree, or succulents without them. Other brands with good gauntlet gloves: West County, Bionic, and Gold Leaf.

Multiple Functions = Simpler Life

I'm all about saving time, money, energy and space, and I love multi-function tools because they save all four! Owning fewer tools with more capabilities saves you money because you only have to buy one tool instead of several. And it saves you time and energy because you can just use the tool in your hand instead of searching for a specific-function tool.

Be warned: many multi-functional tools don't actually do any of their functions well. But the following examples are marvelous exceptions. They also fulfill my pledge to only own tools that are well-made and super strong, so they will last me for years and decades to come.

BRAND LOYALTY: THE SOIL SCOOP

Having been a manufacturer's representative in the garden industry for decades, I have five or six trowels in my toolshed, but I always reach for my Garden Works Soil Scoop first because it replaces so many other tools. A Soil Scoop is great for digging holes, weeding, and even making tiny seed furrows. I love it because its serrated edge makes opening bags of compost or mulch easy, replacing my scissors, which are never there when I need them, whereas I always have my Soil Scoop nearby. The business part of the Soil Scoop is larger than the average trowel, thus it scoops more soil and, most important, saves precious energy. It boasts an easy-to-find, colorful comfort grip handle that is gentle on arthritic hands. Finally, it is approved by

Seniors Select, an organization that approves tools that truly benefit seniors. Finding their seal on a product is a good indication that it will suit your adaptive gardening needs.

Let's Hear It for Hori Hori!

There's nothing quite like a hori hori knife to get the job done. If you don't own one yet, put it on your list when you go shopping. Every gardener who owns one, loves it.

The hori hori knife was created by gardeners in Japan, the word *hori* means "to dig" in Japanese and *hori-hori* is the *onomatopoeia* for the sound of digging.

A good hori hori knife is made of stainless steel, which makes it heavy duty enough to compensate for diminished hand strength when cutting sod or dealing with clay soil, and also means it won't rust. Its blade is heavily serrated on one side and very sharp on both sides.

A hori hori knife does it all, cutting through the toughest, most tangled roots. Be sure to protect the blade and yourself with a sturdy sheath.

This extraordinary multi-purpose tool does so many chores:

☐ *Cuts*

☐ *Saws*

☐ *Digs*

☐ *Weeds*

☐ *Separates*

☐ *Splits*

☐ *Makes a good measuring device for planting bulbs*

The first time I used my hori hori knife, I had to remove some very stubborn clumps of bamboo in my front yard. The knife was unstoppable; I was amazed how easily it cut through those gnarly roots—so much so, I went on to use it to split some overgrown perennials.

TONI'S TIP

The hori hori knife is one of the most useful tools you can buy. Just be careful when you use it. Don't buy one without a well-made leather sheath and be sure to always put it back in its leather sheath for safe-keeping and to prevent accidents. It's super sharp!

Prune Your Plants,
Not Your Pruner Budget

A good quality pruner is your #1 most important gardening tool. Experience shows higher quality pruners hold their sharp edges better, so you work less and save energy while making cuts. Do not try to save money on your pruner. Instead buy the best pruner you can afford.

But with so many pruners available on the market, how do you find the perfect one for you? I can't stress this enough—it's all about comfort. My recommendation is always to purchase hand tools,

A wealth of pruner options!

especially pruners, for their fit and your comfort first and cost last. You use your pruner for longer stretches at a time than any other tool—common sense and cost per use dictate you should buy the best pruner your budget can afford.

When you are looking to buy a new pruner, don't buy it online. There are just too many to choose from and, and you will walk away bleary-eyed and confused, without having a clue which one will work best for you. Instead, start by asking your gardening friends what brand and model pruners they own. Ask them if they are anvil, bypass, or ratchet style and why they like them. Trust me, everyone will have an opinion. Then head out to your local garden center to try out each one of the recommendations.

ROTATING HANDLES

One unique feature you can look for are rotating handles, which allow gardeners suffering from arthritis and fibromyalgia to continue gardening. The rotation follows your hand's natural clenching motion, and arthritic gardeners tell me the rolling action requires far less effort than standard models, reducing fatigue and allowing them to make effortless cuts. It may feel odd at first, but many gardeners find them to be a lifesaver. Brands like Felco, ARS, and Corona all make rotating handles. Try them all out to see which one is best for you.

BRAND LOYALTY: FELCO PRUNERS

There are literally dozens of pruner brands on the market. The most popular brands are: Felco, Fiskars, Corona, ARS, Florian, and Bahco (formerly Sandvik). I'm a Felco fan, and it continues to be my personal favorite. What I love about Felco is, should you drop the tool and chip a blade, their blades and parts are replaceable at the same retailers that sell the pruners. Their steel blades also have a reputation among gardeners for being particularly easy to keep sharp. You can even buy and replace their flexible inner spring, which is part of what makes Felco super easy on your hand (not all pruner springs are as flexible, user-friendly, and easy to replace). They are all ergonomically designed and they are guaranteed for life, so you only have to buy your Felco pruner once. Which is good news because Felco pruners are expensive. They are worth it though. In my experience, when you pay more for a tool, you tend to take better care of it, so it lasts you for years to come.

Felco has twenty-four models to choose from, so to make your shopping easier, here are the best-seller models to look for:

TONI'S TIP

Make sure you determine how thick of a branch you need to cut. Some pruners can only accommodate ⅜ of an inch, while others will work quite effectively at cutting a branch up to 1½ inches thick.

☐ *Felco 2 is by far the most popular of their pruners sold in the United States and worldwide. It is best for gardeners with large hands. There isn't a left-handed version.*

☐ *Felco 6 is lighter than the Felco 2 and is perfect for a small to medium hand. The left-handed version is Felco 16.*

☐ *Felco 8 is very close to the Felco 2 but for medium-sized hands. Felco 9 is the left-handed version of the 8.*

☐ *Felco 12 is designed for heavy-duty use and has a rotating handle that saves wear and tear on the hand. Some people swear by it; others not so much. Try it to see if it will work for you. The left-handed version is Felco 17.*

NEEDLE NOSE

When I am heading out to garden, I always grab my needle nose pruner. Whether you're searching for pups on your succulents or harvesting delicate lettuce leaves, when you need to get into tiny spaces to make your cut, a needle nose pruner is the only way to go. Look for super sharp edges, a non-stick ceramic coating for fast trimming, and an ergonomic non-slip grip. There are many good-quality brands on the market. Shop around and find the most comfortable one— you'll use it a lot and have it a long time.

CUT-AND-HOLD SHORT REACH

The third kind of pruner I recommend is a lightweight short reach pruner with a swivel handle, so you don't have to twist your wrist to make a cut. This tool is ideal for pruning all kinds of plants without bending over and for reaching into thorny shrubs and harvesting roses and lemons. I particularly like cut-and-hold models, because when you cut, they hold on to the trimming so you don't have to bend over to pick it up.

Diamond Tool Sharpeners Are Forever

Even if you invest in good tools, you still need to keep them sharpened. The first tool sharpener I ever bought was from a major brand, but it was only four inches long. I thought to myself, "I'm going to lose this." And I did.

I was determined to find a sharpener I could depend on, so I went to my local nursery and had a conversation with the store manager. She suggested I look for a diamond tool sharpener. Because of their superior quality and the near perfect consistency in their grit size, they get the job done quicker than standard sharpeners.

BRAND LOYALTY: IRONWOOD TOOL SHARPENER

Once I found my 10-inch diamond tool sharpener by Ironwood, I was happy. It has a slip-resistant comfort grip and a safety guard so I can't accidentally cut myself. And it's large enough that I never lose it. I've tried other sharpeners, but I haven't found another one I like as much as this one.

The round, 400-grit coarse side works well for a badly worn or damaged blade edges. Using the flat, 600-grit fine side helps maintain a polished edge. The tapered design allows easy sharpening in between pruner blades where debris can accumulate—with this sharpener, you can clean that area without removing the blades.

Update That Old Saw

In the last few years, I have lost a lot of strength in my hands and arms. A razor-sharp folding saw is the answer to my dilemma. I appreciate being able to saw a branch or a limb with both push and pull strokes—it's 50 percent faster than traditional pull-only razor tooth saws.

For a great saw experience, find one with a comfortable, ergonomic design and, once again, a non-slip comfort grip. The folding model from Wildflower Seed Company really stands out thanks to the safety guard on the handle, which not only helps you to avoid accidents but also protects the blade when the saw is folded and closed.

When in Doubt, Power Up

I heard about this energy-saving tool from Master Gardener Rita Bernardi, who is in a pruning guild. After a talk I did for her group, she told me that when she was learning her new skill, her hands were hurting terribly, so she purchased a cordless lithium battery powered pruner and a hedge trimmer by Teho. Now she prunes without pain and is delighted with her purchase.

When I tried the tools she recommended, I found them to be surprisingly effective at cutting up to a half an inch of green wood. They hold a charge for five hundred cuts before needing to be recharged,

CLOCKWISE
FROM TOP LEFT:
*Hedging is a snap
with a little power
boost.*

*You can power
your way through
most jobs with a
power pruner.*

*Teho sells all these
battery powered
tools as a kit.*

and charging only takes an hour. If you have carpel tunnel, tendon-
itis, or decreased muscle strength in your hands, or if you just want
to shorten your time pruning, give these power tools a try.

Other trusted brands that make battery-powered pruners include
Black and Decker, with its power lopper saw, and both Greenworks
and Gardena's cordless pole hedge trimmer.

BRAND LOYALTY: EARTHWISE LEAF BLOWER

Just like pruning, sweeping and raking can cause back, knee, shoulder, wrist, and hand strain when done over long periods of time.
Until the drought hit here in California, I used a hose in place of a
broom or rake, because it seemed easier. But with water becoming
scarce and prices rising, it was time for a more responsible option.

OPPOSITE:
*Blow off the
hard work with
battery power.*

When I discovered the Earthwise lithium battery leaf blower, my work in the garden became easier. In comparison to the heavy, ill-balanced electric blowers I've tried unsuccessfully over the years, this one does it all. It's efficient enough to blow out all the leaves under my plants, leaving my garden pristine, and it's much quieter than gas-powered blowers.

OPPOSITE: *A truly lightweight hose.*

The Hose Knows

Wrestling with heavy hoses is hard enough for a strong gardener, but when you have a bad back or arthritis, using and storing heavy hoses is literally a pain.

All my original hoses were the wrong hoses. Maybe it was a function of what was available at the time, but still. I was always wrestling with them when I needed them unraveled, unkinked, or back on the hose hanger. Each one was so heavy and awkward to use, it was an easy way to throw out my back. But guess what?

Quality lightweight hoses do exist!

Thankfully, hoses have come a long way. They're lighter, softer, and much gentler on stiff fingers and joints. I like the lightweight options so much, I have replaced all my heavy hoses. Watering is now easy on my body.

Gardeners who live in condos or apartments with patios or lanais and houses with balconies or second-story window boxes will benefit from lightweight coiled hoses because you can attach them to your kitchen faucet with an adapter from your hardware store. Coiled hoses also help prevent injuries that might result from standard hoses, which can be difficult to store.

TONI'S TIP

Buy the shortest hose you need to reach where you will use it. Longer hoses are heavier. Plus, water pressure decreases as hose length increases.

ABOVE: *From a light mist to a powerful force, with just a flick of your thumb.*

OPPOSITE: *An inexpensive siphon mixer eliminates bending over.*

BRAND LOYALTY: THUMB-CONTROLLED HAND SPRAYER

Once you've got a hose you love, you'll want a way to control it. This thumb-controlled hand sprayer from Garden Works USA is Senior Select approved and, unless you have mobility issues with your thumb, super easy to use. You'll appreciate how little pressure you have to apply in order to turn it on, in comparison to a standard hand sprayer.

Ergonomic thumb controlled hand sprayers also make it easy to switch from a soft to a hard spray. The one I use has seven patterns that encompass all the variations I need. It's great when I need to switch from watering large areas in the garden to watering my window boxes, because I can control the flow of water easily and don't have to worry about a too-wide stream accidentally spraying my clean windows.

REEL IT IN

If you're not ready to replace your heavy hoses, why not invest in a retractable garden hose reel? They're available for hoses from 50 to 100 feet long. I used one at my sister's garden and it made short work of using and putting away her hose, so it's not a tripping hazard. All you have to do is give it a little tug and the retracting mechanism does the work for you.

A few brands to investigate: Flo-Master, Gardena, and one whose name says it all, SereneLife Retractable Garden Hose.

TONI'S TIP || Buy the same sprayer for each hose so you never have to think twice about the controls.

Siphon Savior

A siphon mixer is a great product for anyone who loves to fertilize their garden, but can't comfortably bend down to fill up and re-fill a watering can. It's a simple, inexpensive device that saves you precious time and lots of energy. I like the version from Grow More. No matter your garden situation, it could be the key to helping you stay on a regular fertilizing cycle, for a spectacular garden year after year.

Are you an apartment or condo dweller with lots of containers needing regular fertilizer to get lots of blooms? A siphon mixer is definitely a great way to go. This system will assure your garden is as gorgeous as you ever dreamed it—with way less effort.

Add a water-soluble product, such as fish emulsion, Maxsea Plant Food, or Liquinox Bloom to a gallon bucket. Connect your siphon to any outdoor hose bibb and place the bucket underneath. With the end of the siphon in the bucket and using a quick-connect hose attachment, you can easily go from one hose bibb to the next with your lightweight hose, watering wand, and bucket, fertilizing your entire garden without bending over.

RIGHT: *A quick-connect hose attachment makes it easy to move your hose to whichever bibb is most convenient.*

OPPOSITE: *Haws watering cans are simply the best, since 1886.*

The Yes, You Can Cans

If you like to use a watering can, choose carefully. I have owned many watering cans over the years and most of them have leaked at one time or another. It's a frustrating flaw that wastes water— and doesn't it feel like that defeats the can's purpose?

In addition to choosing a can that won't leak, look for one that's well balanced, with easy-to-hold grips, and light enough for your own strength. Many serious gardeners like cans made from galvanized metal, but for me, I find the galvanized cans heavy even when empty. My preference is for cans made of recycled plastic because they are both lighter and easier to use when full *and* they're less expensive.

BRAND LOYALTY: HAWS WATERING CANS

In my experience, the only watering can brand to own is Haws. Their cans have been expertly crafted in England since 1886. I have one that's more than twenty-five years old. It's scratched and nicked up, but guess what? It still never leaks.

As I've aged, I've found it increasingly helpful that Haws watering cans are perfectly balanced—whether you carry them by the handle or by the crossbar. And having the two different hand grips makes for an ergonomic and less tiring carrying and watering position.

Haws offers dozens of models to choose from in a huge selection of styles, shapes, and sizes. I recommend the Long Reach model, but the Practican is also a good one. Both will help you reach across with ease, and have a tall splash-guard, so water doesn't splash out while you're walking.

Stay Comfy and Carry On

BELOW: *A red wagon is as helpful for transporting mulch as it is for grandkids.*

Keeping essential tools with you whenever you go out to the garden saves you time, energy, and aggravation. Think about how many times you have to go back to your garage or toolshed to get something you

forgot. Try incorporating a red wagon, a five gallon bucket, or a handy tote to help you keep tools nearby and prevent you from accidentally losing them or having to make more trips back to the tool shed.

BRAND LOYALTY: STASH-AND-CARRY TOOL SEAT

This product is all about saving time and energy. The Garden Works USA Tool Seat is lightweight yet made from a strong,

foldable steal frame. What is so cool about the Tool Seat is that it comes with its own tool bag that sports lots of pockets, so you'll always have everything you need when you sit down to work in your garden. The tool bag attaches with Velcro and can be used with the tool seat or carried separately. Either way, the seat holds up to 250 pounds.

BRAND LOYALTY: PUDDLE-PROOF TOTE

For years, I have been looking for the perfect tote bag and I finally found it! One of the duties of a Master Gardener is to give back by volunteering at various projects. I personally love to volunteer at work parties, because it's a great way to learn new plants and to meet other members. When I go, I like having a tote for not only all my tools and gloves, but also my water bottle, keys, and phone. This tote is plenty large enough to carry all that, and it's deep enough and long enough to carry my kneeling pad and my Sunset Western Garden Book, which is our bible on the West Coast. It has three pockets on each side, each with an elastic cord so your pruners and tools won't accidentally fall out. And there are mesh pockets on each end that securely hold your water bottles and can be cinched closed with cord locks.

ABOVE LEFT:
Tool Seat with tool bag attached and full of tools.

ABOVE RIGHT:
Tool Seat with tool bag separate. The perfect tote bag ready to go.

It's really well made, so you won't need to replace it for many years. And the best part? The waterproof rubber bottom that keeps everything dry, should you happen to be working next to a puddle.

BRAND LOYALTY: TUFF TOTES

I like using Tuff Totes by Garden Works USA, because they are remarkable for their tough handles—it's those handles that usually break with other brands. What are you going to do besides groan when everything falls on your foot? Tuff Totes have been safety tested to carry up to 225 pounds. You are never going to want to carry that much weight, but the point is they've been tested and can handle anything you might need them for.

BRAND LOYALTY: POTLIFTER

The PotLifter is a great product because it works exactly as advertised. Many of the pots I own are made of concrete. They're super heavy when empty—when you add soil and plants, they're

BELOW LEFT: *Tuff Totes have tough handles.*

BELOW RIGHT: *You can lift all kinds of pots with PotLifter.*

OPPOSITE, *The perfect tote bag ready to go.*

unmovable except with a dolly or the PotLifter. It takes two people to make it happen, but you can move even the heaviest pots with this tool.

BRAND LOYALTY: UPCART LIFT

A friend of mine has stairs in her garden that make it difficult to transport heavy pots. She has a dolly, or hand truck, which works for moving heavy things across flat surfaces, but because the dolly itself is so heavy, it's challenging for getting up stairs without injuring her back.

The six-wheel UpCart makes all the sense in the world for this task. It is well made and well thought out—it is lightweight and sturdy enough to carry up to 200 pounds up and down stairs and over curbs and uneven surfaces. The best part, is that it folds completely flat for easy storage. It's a great tool for saving time, energy, and space.

LEFT: *Finally a good way to get heavy things up and down stairs.*

RIGHT: *After folding, the UpCart is easy to store.*

OPPOSITE: *A great way to effortlessly get around your yard.*

BRAND LOYALTY: TRACTOR SCOOT

I often fantasize about having a larger piece of property and an expansive garden to grow everything I want to grow—then I think about maintaining it, and I'm suddenly awake again! But. If I did have a large garden (and a garage to stow it in), I would own one of these Tractor Scoots from Gardener's Supply Company.

Think of spending an afternoon scooting around your garden with all your tools within reach, as well as a place for bulbs, cuttings, or trash, depending on the chore you are doing. I know a gardener who has a very large yard, with more than six hundred rose bushes, and her tractor scoot allows her to move from one bush to the next easily, making her dead-heading and maintenance a snap.

What Your Knees Need

Even with lots of modifications and nifty tools designed to help you garden standing up, you might still need or want to get down on your knees and garden at ground level. Fortunately there are lots of gadgets available to make this experience comfortable and safe.

REVERSIBLE KNEELER SEAT

Getting down is the easy part . . . getting back up, not so much! Gardeners of any age can appreciate a reversible kneeler seat. There are several good brands on the market, but I like the one from Bosmere. See it in action in the photos below.

I like it so much, I have two; one for the front yard, another the back. I always keep one next to our raised beds, so I don't have to lean over to work. If you buy one, I can guarantee it will become one of your most indispensable tools.

BRAND LOYALTY: KOMFY KNEES

I am not sure who designed them, but the first pair of knee pads I bought had a velcro strap that passed right across the back of the knee, so when I kneeled down with them on, they hurt! Sometimes I wonder what product designers are thinking!

Then I found a product called Komfy Knees from Garden Works. They are super lightweight and comfortable neoprene kneepads—a gardener's dream. Their designers were smart, positioning the velcro straps to go around your leg above your knee and below it, no uncomfortable strap scrunching or rubbing. As an added bonus, they are waterproof, washable, and approved by Senior Select.

BRAND LOYALTY: BOSNEELEZE

I love memory foam so I am always open to checking out products that utilize it. I recently found this thick and super lightweight kneeling pad from Bosmere and was pleased with how comfortable it was to use. This is not your everyday kneeler. It's waterproof,

BELOW LEFT:
Memory foam to help you forget knee pain.

BELOW RIGHT:
Smart knee pads with velcro in the right place.

washable, super easy on your knees, and can withstand even your muddiest frolicking. You can kneel down to work in your garden all day without worrying about the pad getting trashed.

Clean up

Once you've pruned, weeded, swept, and raked using all your comfy new tools, you'll need to clean up all the resulting debris. All my adaptive gardening advice thus far won't be much use if you throw your back out on this last step. The following tools are here to help.

YELLOW THING

I know you are asking . . . what the heck is a "yellow thing"?

Well, that's what my husband and I call it. Manufacturers call it a Jumbo Debris Pan. We find it invaluable whenever we're sweeping or raking up clippings and weeds around the garden, because you don't have to bend down to use it. When it's full, you can lift it off the ground and it goes from being horizontal to vertical so no debris falls out. You can find a yellow thing of your very own at most hardware stores or at Home Depot where it is a staple.

BRAND LOYALTY: BOS BAG

Your yellow thing is good for scooping things up, but if you have a lot of debris, you'll need to make multiple trips to your green bin. Unless you have a Bos Bag by Bosmere close by.

When I discovered Bos Bag, I thought to myself: "Why haven't I see this before?" It's a debris collector made of non-tear polyethylene, so it weighs absolutely nothing. While you're working, it sits up and

stays open, thanks to the wires inside the lining. When it's full, the handles make it easy to transport your debris to your green can. And the coolest part? It folds flat for easy storage.

The dream team in action. Bos Bag plus yellow thing is a winning comBINation.

GO SHOPPING

Ten things to keep in mind when you go out shopping for new tools:

1 Buy the best quality tool you can afford for the type of gardening you do.

2 Try the tool before you buy the tool. Ask the retailer if you can handle the product outside of its packaging so you can determine if it's a good fit for your hand. If they refuse, go to another store.

3 How is the grip? Does it fit your hand well? Is it comfortable? The "best" tool in the world will not work for you if it's too large or small, too heavy, or uncomfortable to hold.

4 Look for an ergonomic tool that keeps your wrist in a neutral alignment.

5 The handle should be big enough so your thumb barely overlaps your fingers.

6 Tools with trigger grips and rounded-out thumb rests are easier and more comfortable to hold.

7 If it will require cleaning, determine if it's easy to disassemble.

8 Make sure it's lightweight and balanced. Stainless steel tools can be heavy, especially if you have arthritis or decreased muscle strength in your hands. Galvanized watering cans are heavy when they are empty. Look for ones made from metal alloys or strong plastics.

9 Long reach tools are just the ticket when your back or shoulder is aching.

10 Many tools come with a warranty or guarantee. Some retailers may let you try it in your garden and return it if it doesn't work for you. Remember to file away the receipt, just in case.

When your grandkids ask you what you want for your birthday . . .

Parting Thoughts

Here are some things I learned while writing this book:

We will continue to age.

We must learn to accept it.

*We can adapt now for
the future.*

*We get by with the help
of our friends.*

*We create community
when we garden together.*

We can garden for life.

*It is a wonderful world,
when you can keep doing
what you love to do, for as long
as you want to do it!*

It is my sincere hope I helped you feel like no matter what you're going through, you can find new ways to be creative and resilient, because there is always another way to get it done. I hope you look for and find ease and joy on your adaptive gardening path. Keep gardening. Never give up.

Con amore (with love),
Toni

Adaptive Gardening Action Plan

GARDENER, KNOW THYSELF:
What physical issues do you experience when you garden?

_____

_____

_____

_____

_____

_____

What garden chores have become painful to do? Which can
you delegate?

_____

_____

_____

_____

_____

_____

What habits can you change now for greater comfort and joy as
you continue gardening?

_____

_____

_____

_____

_____

_____

RE-ENVISION YOUR GARDEN

Plan changes for easier maintenance and sustainability. Check all possible adaptations that apply to your garden:

Change hardscape for mobility

☐ *Eliminate gaps and tripping-hazard transitions*

☐ *Make paths 4 feet wide and a solid surface*

☐ *Replace stairs with a ramp*

☐ *Add fencing*

☐ *Incorporate raised beds, containers, and vertical gardens*

Downsize and simplify for ease

☐ *Replace annuals & perennials with shrubs and trees*

☐ *Replace the lawn*

☐ *Add drought-resistant native plants*

☐ *Install drip irrigation with a timer*

☐ *Create a wildlife habitat*

☐ *Compost and mulch*

☐ *Avoid pesticides*

☐ *Right plant, right place*

- [ ] *Utilize integrated pest management (IPM)*

- [ ] *Let your garden naturalize*

TOOL TIME

Find the perfect tools to increase your comfort and save you energy.

What tools can you adapt?

_____

_____

_____

_____

_____

_____

_____

_____

What tools do you want to buy?

_____

_____

_____

_____

_____

_____

_____

_____

Resources

PROGRAMS TO BUILD YOUR STRENGTH AND RESILIENCE

DynamicVitality.com

Fallproof.com

Go4Life.nia.nih.gov (from the National
  Institute on Aging at NIH)

Healthyagingassociation.
  org/a-matter-of-balance

Steppingon.com

BOOKS ON RESILIENCE AND JOY

*Rising Strong: How the Ability to Reset
  Transforms the Way We Live, Love,
  Parent, and Lead* by Brené Brown

*The Book of Joy: Lasting Happiness in a
  Changing World* by Dalai Lama and
  Desmond Tutu

Tribe: On Homecoming and Belonging by
  Sebastian Junger

The Four Agreements by don Miguel Ruiz

The Five Levels of Attachment by don
  Miguel Ruiz Jr.

*The Untethered Soul: The Journey Beyond
  Yourself* by Michael A. Singer

Acknowledgements

Thanks to the following locations:

Annie's Annuals, Richmond, CA
Cornerstone Sonoma-Sunset Test Gardens, Sonoma, CA
Marin Art & Garden Center, Ross, CA
Harvey's Garden, Blackie's Pasture, Tiburon, CA

Photo Credits

All photos courtesy of Heidi Hornberger unless indicated below.

Audubon Canyon Ranch, page 33
Cobrahead LLC, page 158 (right)
Connie Pelissero, page 81
Creative Commons, CC0, page 44
Gardeners Supply, pages 123, 137, 143 (left), 144, 168 (left), 177, 178, 186, 189
HGTV, page 133
Kathy Jentz, page 143 (right)
Kathy Hunting © 2018 UC Regents, page 77
Pale Trading Co., page 187 (right)
Easy Container Combos: Herbs and Flowers by Pamela Crawford, page 136 (left)
Pinebush Home and Garden, page 161
Susan Morrison, pages 101, 136 (bottom right)
Fairfax Image Photography, page 7

123RF
denisfilm, page 196 (top right)

GAP
Clive Nichols, pages 92 (right), 135
GAP Photos, pages 84, 124 (right), 126
Lynn Keddie, page 120

ISTOCK
49pauly, page 22 (bottom right)
CampPhoto, page 95
croquette, page 170
Eivaisla, page 8
Emmeci74, page 3
EvaKaufman, page 78
FangXiaNuo, page 27
fotolotos, page 2
Gannet77, page 82
Halfpoint, page 20
HannamariaH, page 87

imv, page 5 (left)

Karla Ferro, page 18

KatarzynaBialasiewicz, page 91

KenWiedmemann, page 140

oversnap, page 204

phanasitti, page 141 (top left)

PictureLake, page 106

susannahphotography, page 45

Thomas Shanahan, page 196 (top left)

uuurska, page 117

wayra, page 141 (right)

SHUTTERSTOCK

Alina G, page 74

Anne Greenwood, page 124 (left)

Backyarder, page 141 (bottom left)

Bildagentur Zoonar GmbH, page 196
(bottom right)

Bonnie Taylor Berry, pages 128–129

Byjeng, page 104 (left)

Chukov, page 111 (right)

Del Boy, page 128

Ed Samuel, page 132 (right)

Hannamariah, page 134

In This Instance, page 111 (left)

Ivonne Wierink, page 127

Kristen Prahl, page 5 (right)

Linda Bestwick, page 26

Lydia Vero, page 4 (left)

Monkey Business Images, page 75

Montri Thipsom, page 41

olenaa, page 29

riopatuca, page 89 (left)

romakoma, page 104 (right)

Shyntartanya, page 198

Simon Tang, page 116, 22 (left)

Skyler Ewing, page 22 (top)

Somchai Siriwanarangson, page 4
(right)

Tulia Grigoryeva, page 48

Zivica Kerkez, page 73

Index

THE LIFELONG GARDENER

About the Author

TONI GATTONE'S PASSION FOR GARDENING began in her Italian grandfather's backyard in Chicago. In 1990, after an accomplished career in sales, her entrepreneurial spirit and gardening passion took over, and she opened the doors to Toni Gattone & Associates, a successful wholesale sales organization, selling gift and garden products to retailers throughout California and Northern Nevada.

In 2011, Toni became a UC certified Master Gardener in Marin County, CA. Her persistent bad back motivated her to develop and deliver her informative talk, *You Can Garden for Life with Adaptive Gardening*. Toni and her husband Tim King live in Larkspur, CA, where they have converted their traditional ornamental front yard into an adapted edible landscape.

Heidi Hornberger